To Winnie and Dick,

With fondest best

wishes,

Claudia and Donald

May 1989

**The Robert H. Clague Collection
Chinese Glass of the Qing Dynasty**

Phoenix Art Museum
21 Nov 1987 - 31 Jan 1988

San Antonio Museum of Art
18 March - 19 June 1988

Suntory Museum of Art, Tokyo
19 Jul - 28 Aug 1988

Milwaukee Public Museum
21 Jan - 16 Apr 1989

This exhibition catalog and the
international tour have been
underwritten by generous grants
from Mr and Mrs John Cotton
and an anonymous donor.

Claudia Brown and Donald Rabiner

The Robert H. Clague Collection

Chinese Glass of the Qing Dynasty
1644-1911

Phoenix Art Museum 1987

Published by the
Phoenix Art Museum
1625 N. Central Avenue
Phoenix, AZ 85004-1685

Photography:
Steven Tucker

Additional Photography:
Bob Carey - 15, 16, 60, 62, 75,
76, 77, 78-81 and marks 2,
13, 17, 28, 29, 35, 36, 39, 40, 43,
45, 53, 57
Chuck Garner - 73; mark 15
National Palace Museum,
Taipei and
Palace Museum, Beijing

Design:
Thomas Detrie and
Karen Hayes-Thumann

Composition:
Typography Unlimited, Inc.

Lithography:
Prisma Graphic Corp.

Library of Congress
catalog card number:
87-42927
For CIP Data see p. 96

ISBN 0-910407-20-7

Contents

James K. Ballinger
Director
Phoenix Art Museum

Preface

In 1980 the Phoenix Art Museum organized an exhibition of Chinese cloisonné from the collection of Robert H. Clague. Since that time the cloisonné has become part of the museum's permanent collection, the acclaimed exhibition has been seen in thirteen cities throughout the country, and Mr Clague has begun anew to collect in a little-studied field of Chinese decorative arts. Glass, whose vitreous composition differs little from the enamels of cloisonné, fittingly succeeds cloisonné as the object of his acute attention.

In the decade since Phelps Warren complained of the paucity of studies on later Chinese glass, the publication of numerous pieces has provided a significant pool for study. While little new information has appeared in Western studies, Chinese scholars have addressed themselves increasingly to this area, prompted by intense archeological activity as well as growing interest in the Qing imperial collections housed now in Beijing and Taipei. The present catalog, by presenting for the first time in English articles on glass by a scholar at the Palace Museum, Beijing, and a scholar at the National Palace Museum, Taipei, seeks to bring fresh insight to the study of later Chinese glass. Three scholars in this country, Dr James Watt of the Metropolitan Museum, Dr Robert Brill at the Corning Museum, and Professor Ju-hsi Chou of Arizona State University, provided comments which have been most useful in the editing and adaptation of these two articles.

Many have helped with the documentation of the Robert Clague collection over the years. Winberta Yao of the University Libraries, Arizona State University, provided bibliographical assistance. Working translations and interpretations of inscriptions were supplied by Pei-hsien Wu, Wai-fong Anita Siu and Joseph Wang. Preliminary study of some works in the collection was undertaken by Ruth Shaw as a part of her thesis for the BA degree at North Staffordshire Polytechnic. A special remembrance is due to Miriam Kinner, once the owner of several pieces now in the Clague collection, who shared her enthusiasm for Chinese glass with many in the Phoenix and Sun City area.

The Museum is grateful to Professor Donald Rabiner of the Art History faculty at Arizona State University, for his collaboration on this catalogue with Claudia Brown, our Curator of Asian Art. Dr Brown's exhibitions and publications have brought great attention to the Museum's Asian collections during the past several years. We are very pleased that Robert Clague shares our vision, and special thanks are due to Amy Clague for her enthusiastic support of this project.

Claudia Brown
Donald Rabiner

Introduction

The use of glass in ancient China as a substitute for jade and an embellishment for bronze has long been known to art historians.[1] Following the pioneering studies of W. B. Honey,[2] however, most have come to doubt the continuity of Chinese glassmaking from ancient times to the modern period. Ironically, even as scholars have accepted the convincing arguments for re-attributing most post-Han glass to the seventeenth century and later, archeologists in China have been turning up impressive examples of the craft in sites from the Northern Wei, Sui, Tang, Song, Yuan, and Ming.[3] These important finds leave no doubt of a continuous, if not always flourishing, tradition of glassmaking in China.

Our knowledge of later Chinese glass is based on Chinese texts and archival documents, on Western sources including eighteenth and nineteenth century travelers' commentaries, on analogies of shape and decoration to more studied fields such as ceramics, jade, and lacquer, and on analysis of archeologically excavated glass objects. This last approach promises to reveal much about the development of Chinese glass in the post-Song era.[4]

Despite the currency of such terms as 'Peking' glass, it remains difficult to associate specific types of glass with known places of manufacture: the Palace Workshop and the commercial glasshouses of Beijing, Boshan (Shandong Province), and Guangzhou (Canton).[5] Textual references can be tantalizing. For example, descriptions of Guangzhou glass as 'thin and brittle' tempt one to attribute thinly made pieces such as 33 in the present catalog to the Guangzhou glassmakers. On the other hand, certain unusual types of glass, like the highly sculptural style of 69, cannot yet be linked with a specific studio. The collecting and exhibition of later Chinese glass, until recently sporadic, will aid in the process of understanding regional developments.[6]

The establishment of imperial workshops in the late seventeenth century set into motion a rich interaction among the crafts. Glassmaking had long encompassed the imitation of hardstones, but now, working side by side with lacquerers, enamelers, and jade craftsmen, glassmen took inspiration from other crafts. Shapes were drawn from ceramics, lacquer, and jade, decoration from porcelain and lacquer. Even after imperial patronage declined to an insignificant level, the interplay between the crafts continued to flourish. After the cutback in the Palace Workshop in the second half of the eighteenth century, private patrons eager to emulate the court's luxury supported commercial glassmakers who took up many of the techniques and decorative schemes in use at the court.

Although foreign craftsmen were assigned to the Palace Workshop, the influence of their European glass-making techniques has been overstated by Western scholars. Yang Boda's study published below suggests that the most active participation of foreigners in glassmaking at court took place in the 1740's and 1750's. Not only did the formula for glass change but the archives record the enrollment of European craftsmen to fabricate Western-style flowers and chandeliers, many of which were destined for use in the Western-style buildings of the Yuanming Yuan summer palace. Père Amiot, writing in 1752, described a small 'machine', erected by the Jesuits on the grounds of the Yuanming Yuan, in the form of a theater three feet high set within a 'basin' of mirror glass.[7] Jets of water fashioned of lamp-worked glass were so well constructed, he wrote, that 'they fooled one even from close up.' Regarding earlier European contributions to Chinese glassmaking, Père Benoît noted in 1773 that a secular glassman (neither priest nor lay brother) had served at court for

Numbers refer
to catalog entries

a number of years during the Kangxi reign (1662-1722).[8] Nevertheless, however much technical assistance the European craftsmen may have lent, few surviving pieces of Chinese glass owe a discernible debt to European styles. The exceptions are those in which striping (Yang, figure 5) or 'twined-silk' decoration is derived from Venetian types. Clear or yellow ice grounds (24, 28, 29) are often said to imitate Venetian *vetro a ghiaccio* or ice glass, but comparison of the two types shows little similarity. Examples in which the vessel shape derives from European sources are exceedingly few, while most forms seem to stem directly from ceramics, especially the monochrome ceramics which came to be a preoccupation of the court-sponsored porcelain kilns. Numbers 1 and 3 are based on contemporary ceramic shapes and echo the monochrome blue and 'ox-blood' red glazes of Kangxi porcelain. These vessels suggest that one role of glass may have been to create a transparent pseudo-porcelain, as if the glaze had taken over the role of the clay body to produce a wholly diaphanous vessel.

The interaction of ceramics and glass resulted in fruitful experimentation throughout the Qing period. The Song and Yuan dynasty celadon tradition provided sources for glass shapes in its mallet vases (43) and foliate dishes (55). And the celadon glaze color, itself associated with blue-green jade, provided inspiration for monochrome opaque glass (35). Surface painting in gold or enamel was a decorative practice shared by monochrome glass and porcelain. Gilt decoration was applied to glazed monochrome stoneware and porcelain during the Song dynasty, and gained renewed currency in late Ming and Qing ceramics. During the Qianlong (1736-95), and perhaps as late as the Jiaqing (1796-1820) period, gilt decoration was applied to transparent as well as opaque glass grounds (48). Enamel decoration of the *yangcai* ('foreign colors' or *famille rose*) type, distinguished by its use of a tin-oxide opacifier to allow for shading, unites enamelled glass, typically of opaque white ground (49, 50), with enamelled porcelain. The technique arose during the second or third decade of the eighteenth century, and retained its prominence into the twentieth century.[9] The rose-pink of the *yangcai* palette became a body color for monochrome glass; sometimes this was a dusty-rose hue (73) not unlike the rose enamel of Tongzhi period (1862-74) porcelain.

Glassmakers throughout the ancient world produced simulated precious stones. In Europe this practice eventually became only a minor aspect of glassmaking, but in China, because of the special appreciation of jade and other hardstones, the imitation of stone became a major feature of later glass. Convincing imitations of jade, occasionally mistaken for the mineral itself, survive in great quantity. Press-molded wine cups (74), usually with molded decoration of *shou* (long-life) characters, may have been burial items. Coarsely finished and with prominent mold seams, they are likely to have served as less expensive substitutes for jade in a context where finish was of little consequence.[10] Small glass toggles and plaques (82-90) imitating jade were made in the Ming and Qing dynasties.[11]

Gold, in ancient times associated with the cult of immortality, was imitated in aventurine glass, which may have been imported from Europe before being produced at the Qing court. Gold-flecked blue glass, imitating lapis lazuli, appears prominently in Kangxi-period descriptions of glass. Realgar, a mineral with strong alchemical associations, inspired the mottled red, orange, and yellow pieces (40) made as early as the first half of the eighteenth century.[12] Other minerals may have been imitated purely for the beauty of their colors, as were malachite (20), turquoise (43-47), and carnelian (42). Glass imitations of amber (12, 14, 15) were especially common. Color and texture at times were both imitated, as in the case of coral (41). Glass substitutes for semi-precious stones often were used as inlays in various types of metalwork.

Of all the methods of working glass, the lapidary approach is the most characteristically Chinese. Since neolithic times, the working of jades with tools and abrasives had been a fundamental aspect of Chinese art. Under the imperial patronage of the mid-Qing, the carving of glass with relief decoration came into prominence. Cutting away the surface to form facets (see the Kangxi-marked piece illustrated below in Yang, figure 1) or flutes (Yang, figure 2) may have been one of the earliest styles of glass carving. The crisply articulated concave fluting of Qianlong-period examples (5) calls to mind the comment of the nineteenth-century connoisseur Zhao Zhiqian that Qianlong glass had 'detail as fine as hair and a ridge discernible to the touch.'[13] Fluting and faceting continued as decorative techniques into the nineteenth and twentieth centuries (53, 61).

Another innovation that can be documented to the Kangxi era was cased or overlay glass, which Western scholars have been reluctant to place before the Qianlong era.[14] This technique could be used to enhance the color of plain monochromes (58),[15] but more often casing was combined with lapidary work to produce the distinctive carved overlay or cameo glass so closely associated with the Chinese tradition. The practice has many parallels in other Chinese decorative arts: the working of jade so as to make decorative or pictorial use of the brown 'skin' of the pebble; the carving of multicolored layers of lacquer, used to great pictorial effect during the Ming dynasty; and even the working of hornbill, an organic material which was typically carved to make the best decorative or pictorial use of its outer red layer (for glass imitations of this material see 28, 29).

Casing permitted a wide range of coloristic effects. The ground could be of clear glass, sometimes clouded with pinpoint specks (like the snow or ice ground of 24) or speckled with additional colors (19). Experimentation with casing in multiple colors during the first half of the eighteenth century seems to be reflected in 20-23. The brilliant rose-pink of 21 is accompanied by an overlay of white under transparent blue, and several of the overlaid colors on the transparent grounds of the other pieces are veined as if in imitation of agate or other semi-precious stones. Under court patronage the overlay process was combined with imperial imagery and archaistic motifs, often applied to a yellow-tinged ground suggesting ivory (17, 18, and Yang, figure 8). Sometimes a semi-translucent ground similar to mutton-fat jade was used to set off transparent overlays (27, 62), or the white ground was striated (26). White-ground overlay glass from the nineteenth century seems to lack these variations, and a uniform opaque white prevails (for example, 25, 34). Variations in overlay also diminish, so that most consist simply of one opaque color (often blue or red) over a white ground.

Relief carving flourished in the eighteenth century. Transparent monochromes were either mold-blown or cased to form a thick body, and then carved with motifs like birds-and-flowers (13), children at play (6), and archaistic dragons (15). Some pieces of this period were so deeply carved that the craftsman risked breaking the glass (16). Rich sculptural effects could be achieved in the carving of overlays (27).

Techniques of wheel-engraving (75), stippling (14), and etching (12) were practiced at court in the eighteenth century and sporadically later on. Of special note are the finely engraved poetic inscriptions which must have been carried out by jade carvers from the imperial studios. These seem to have enjoyed a particular vogue in the later eighteenth century (38, 39), and take as their texts imperial compositions by the Qianlong emperor or poetic works by high officials.[16]

Later Chinese glass is notoriously difficult to date. Western scholars tend to distinguish eighteenth-century (and particularly Qianlong) glass from later productions on the basis of quality, viewing nineteenth-century glass (like the porcelain, jade, cloisonné, and other decorative arts of that century) as technically deficient and lacking in innovation. As recent studies of late Qing porcelain have shown, however, the quality of nineteenth-century decorative arts at times could attain an exceptionally high level. Nevertheless, we do possess documentary evidence that at least within the imperial workshop the quality and scale of glass production declined after the mid-to-late eighteenth century, and it seems reasonable to accept the rule-of-thumb which associates glass of high quality with the eighteenth century.

Fortunately, this is not the only criterion for dating. The technical defect known as crizzling, caused by an excess of alkali in the batch, usually is associated with glass of the late seventeenth and early eighteenth centuries, and is exhibited here in several pieces including 1 and 8.[17] Another feature of the former associated with an early date is the application of a cane of glass to form a coiled ring foot,[18] and its rather ungainly shape is found as well in ceramics of the Kangxi era. In general, bubbles and foreign inclusions suggest a date before the nineteenth century. So too, as noted above, do variation rather than uniformity in color, and crisp carving of facets and ribs (compare 5 and 53). In terms of carving, particularly of overlays, nineteenth-century glass often exhibits only a single plane of relief supplemented with incisions for details, in contrast to the more sculptural modelling of the eighteenth century. These provisional rules-of-thumb await the confirmation of further study, which no doubt will provide a firmer basis for dating Chinese glass.

Although glass may be only a small aspect of later Chinese decorative art, Qing dynasty connoisseurs were enthusiastic about its charms. The poet Wang Shizhen's praise of glass as 'clear as crystal, red as flame'[19] calls to mind the intensity of early eighteenth-century transparent monochrome glass. As opaque monochrome colors came to rival the semi-precious stones they imitated, and as jade craftsmen came to exploit a material at once easier to work and more brilliant in coloristic effect, no less an esthete than Zhao Zhiqian[20] could exclaim over the radiance, the precise carving and the archaic resonance of the finest Qing glass.

Notes

1 A spectacular example of glass embellishment of bronze is the Winthrop mirror (see Max Loehr, *Ancient Chinese Jades* [Cambridge, MA, 1975], no. 524). The Winthrop collection includes a number of examples of glass substitutes for jade (nos. 541-44 and 566). More rare is the use of glass inlay in gold (nos. 474-75).

2 The trend began with the publication of two key articles by W. B. Honey: 'Early Chinese Glass,' *Burlington Magazine* 71 (1937): 221-22, and 'Chinese Glass,' *Transactions of the Oriental Ceramics Society* 18 (1939-40): 35-47.

3 See the survey article by An Jiayao, 'Zhongguo de zaoqi boli qimin' (Early glass vessels of China), *Kaogu xuebao* (1984, no.4): 413-48. A 1984 symposium in Beijing was devoted to the scientific analysis of Chinese glass from earliest times to the modern era. The proceedings are available in Chinese (see bibliography), with an English language edition forthcoming, to be published by the Corning Museum of Glass. The authors are grateful to Robert Brill of the Corning Museum of Glass for making available English texts of papers presented at the symposium.

4 See for example Zibo Municipal Museum, 'Zibo Yuan mo Ming chu bolizuofang yizhi' (Excavation of a glass workshop dating from the late Yuan and early Ming in Zibo city), *Kaogu* (1985, no.6): 530-39.

5 That Guangzhou produced pieces worthy of the imperial court is demonstrated in the essays which follow. Not only were craftsmen recruited in Guangzhou, but locally made glass objects were included among the tribute items sent to the court. See Yang Boda, 'The Characteristics and Status of Guangdong Handicrafts as Seen from 18th Century Tributes from Guangdong in the Collection of the Former Qing Palace,' in *Tributes from Guangdong to the Qing Court* (Art Gallery, Chinese University of Hong Kong, 1987).

6 The Victoria and Albert and British Museums in London, the City of Bristol Museum and Art Gallery, the Museum for Far Eastern Antiquities in Stockholm, the Royal Ontario Museum in Toronto, the Museum of Fine Arts in Boston, the Asian Art Museum in San Francisco, the Toledo Museum of Art, and the Tokyo National Museum have accumulated significant pieces of later Chinese glass which have yet to be fully documented. Notable progress is shown by such scholarly efforts as Doris Dohrenwend, 'Glass in China: A Review Based on the Collection in the Royal Ontario Museum,' *Oriental Art* 26 (1980-81): 426-46. Chemical analysis of selected pieces in the Boston Museum of Fine Arts was undertaken by P. England, J.C.Y. Watt, and L.V. Zelst (see the proceedings of the 1984 symposium cited in the bibliography). Of special importance are two recent exhibitions of Chinese glass. The first was organized by the Museum für Kunsthandwerk, Frankfurt, with catalogue by Gunhild Gabbert, *Chinesisches Glas* (Frankfurt, 1980). The second was organized by the Suntory Museum of Art, with the catalogue *Kenryū garasu to āru nūvō* (Tokyo, 1983).

7 *Lettres édifiantes et curieuses, écrites des missions etrangères*, 2nd ed. (Paris, 1781-83), 23: 154.

8 *Lettres édifiantes et curieuses*, 24: 311.

9 So much associated with the Qing court was it that the imperial pretender Yuan Shikai, during his brief reign in 1916 commissioned many glass and ceramic pieces in this style.

10 Many of these cups have appeared on the market of late, prompting speculation of fakery. Those in the Bishop White collection at Toronto were collected early this century (see Dohrenwend, 'Glass in China,' figure 31). The authors are indebted to James Watt of the Metropolitan Museum for his comments on this type.

11 On toggles, see Schuyler Cammann, *Substance and Symbol in Chinese Toggles* (Philadelphia, 1962).

12 Because of its alchemical associations, realgar, a poisonous material whose lack of uniformity makes it ill-suited for carving, nevertheless was used for small sculptures of Taoist immortals. The associations of glass with immortality and with both Taoism and Buddhism (glass – or possibly rock crystal – vessels often appear in Buddhist paintings) need further exploration. For an imitation-realgar vase in the British Museum and bowl in the Metropolitan Museum, see Warren, 'Later Chinese Glass,' figs. 50-51.

13 Zhao Zhiqian, *Yonglu xianjie,* in *Meishu congshu,* first *ji, ji* 3: 215.

14 Contrast the evidence in Yang below with the conclusion of Peter H. Plesch, 'Some Approaches to the Study of Later Chinese Glass,' in *Festschrift für Wilhelm Meister,* ed. Annaliese Ohm and Horst Reber, Hamburg, 1975, p. 79: 'The fact that reign-marks earlier than that of the Ch'ien-lung Emperor are not found on overlay glasses is fair enough evidence that this technique originated in that period.'

15 By contrast to casing, the addition of a thin overlayer to tint a body of clear glass is called flashing. Flashing with red (see cat. no. 57) seems to have been particularly common, perhaps as a means to retain a degree of transparency that would be lost in thick walled pieces of this dense color.

16 Other examples bearing inscriptions of poetry by the Qianlong emperor are illustrated in *Arts of the Ch'ing Dynasty,* (exh. cat., London, 1964), pl. 106, no. 326; *Kenryū garasu,* p.26, no. 115; and Warren, 'Later Chinese Glass,' figure 36. An example with an inscription of a text by the official Dong Gao appeared at auction (Sotheby's, New York, sale of 28 February 1980, lot 156). James Watt has suggested in a private communication that the cutbacks at the Palace Workshops may have put jade-carvers out of work, leaving them free to improvise such types as this.

17 Whether this feature can be linked to the experimentation with European formulas remains to be shown (see Yang below and Warren, 'Later Chinese Glass,' 88). The ongoing studies at the Corning Museum of Glass, particularly the work of Robert Brill, no doubt will shed light on this question.

18 See Warren, 'Later Chinese Glass,' 93.

19 Wang Shizhen, *Xiangzu biji,* in *Biji xiaoshuo daguan,* twenty-eighth *bian,* 5: 3054-55.

20 Zhao Zhiqian, *Yonglu xianjie,* 214.

1 Large Vase
crizzled translucent blue
h 47.6 cm (18¾ in)
late 17th century

Tall vase with elongated neck and flared mouth above ovoid body, the applied rope foot formed by a thick coil of glass (see detail). Crizzled surface with swirling stria. Relatively thin-walled; originally transparent light blue.

For a similar piece, formerly Eumorfopoulos collection, now in the Victoria and Albert Museum (C161-1938), see R. Soame Jenyns, *Chinese Art*, rev. ed., ed. William Watson (New York, 1982), vol. 3, fig. 79, and Phelps Warren, 'Later Chinese Glass,' *Journal of Glass Studies* 19 (1977), fig. 8.

The Robert H. Clague Collection

2 Large Vase
transparent red
h 25.7 cm (10⅛ in)
Qianlong mark and period (1736-95)

The globular body surmounted by a tall, thick cylindrical neck, the base slightly recessed. Scattered bubbles and inclusions throughout. Carved four-character reign mark 'Qianlong nian zhi' on base.

3 Vase
transparent red
h 20 cm (7⅞ in)
Yongzheng mark and period (1723-35)

Pear-shaped body with tapering cylindrical neck. Numerous air bubbles and dirt inclusions. Considerable wear on shallow recessed base. Slight crizzling of interior. Four-character reign mark 'Yongzheng nian zhi' incised in double square on base.

4 Alms Bowl
transparent red
d 16.5 cm (6½ in)
Qianlong mark and period (1736-95)

The rounded sides rise from a slightly recessed base to an incurved mouth. Thick body, considerable wear on foot. The base carved with the six-character reign mark 'Da Qing Qianlong nian zhi' in seal script.

5 Fluted Vase
transparent blue
h 24.5 cm (9⅝ in)
Qianlong mark and period (1736-95)

Fluted pear-shaped vase with tall neck and flaring foot, the twelve flutes crisply defined. Squared four-character reign mark 'Qianlong nian zhi' carved in relief in seal script on base.

Formerly H. G. Beasley collection.

6 Lobed Bowl
carved transparent red
d 14.3 cm (5⅝ in)
Qianlong mark but possibly early 19th century

Five-lobed bowl with everted rim. Three lobes carved with floral design, two with small boys with bird and dog. Small air bubbles throughout. Recessed foot ring with incised four-character reign mark 'Qianlong nian zhi' in double square.

7 Bowl
transparent blue
d 16.2 cm (6⅜ in)
Qianlong period (1736-95)

Deep blue bowl with rounded sides and slightly everted lip, on a recessed foot ring. Elongated air bubbles throughout. Originally painted in gold with phoenix and dragon on exterior, dragon amidst scrolling foliage on interior, and four-character Qianlong mark on base.

8 Shallow Bowl
translucent blue
d 17 cm (6¾ in)
first half 18th century

Shallow bowl with everted rim and slightly recessed ring foot. The irregular glass clouded by slight crizzling and with many small bubbles and inclusions.

9 Large Vase
transparent blue
h 26.7 cm (10½ in)
Qianlong mark and period (1736-95)

Bulbous bottom with large flaring neck and recessed ring foot. Elongated air bubbles. Incised four-character reign mark 'Qianlong nian zhi' in double square on base.

For a similar piece in the Metropolitan Museum of Art, see Warren, 'Later Chinese Glass,' fig. 27.

10 Gourd-shaped Vase
transparent blue
h 23.5 cm (9¼ in)
Qianlong mark and period (1736-95)

Vase of double-gourd shape with gently tapering neck and shallow recessed base. Deep transparent blue suffused with bubbles. Carved four-character reign mark 'Qianlong yu zhi' in single square on base.

11 Large Vase
transparent blue
h 37.8 cm (14⅞ in)
second half 18th century

Globular body with tall cylindrical neck and slightly flared foot. Body relatively thick. Evidence of carving at join between neck and body. Waxy surface.

12 Bowl
transparent amber with wheel-cut and etched decoration
d 14.5 cm (5¾ in)
Qianlong mark and period (1736-95)

The interior of bowl deeply recessed into ring foot. Exterior surface decoration (possibly added later) with two panels of wheel-cut decoration against an etched ground and reserved floral sprays, and additional floral sprays outside panels executed in reverse technique. Thick body suffused with air bubbles and inclusions. Four-character reign mark 'Qianlong nian zhi' carved in single square on base.

13 Bowl
carved transparent green
d 15.5 cm (6⅛ in)
Qianlong mark and period (1736-95)

Bowl with flaring sides and everted rim, the interior slightly recessed into ring foot. Outer surface well carved with pair of phoenix with rock and camellia. Extremely fine air bubbles throughout. Four-character reign mark 'Qianlong nian zhi' incised in bold square on base.

14 Bowl
transparent amber with stippled reserves
d 20 cm (7⅞ in)
Qianlong mark and period (1736-95)

Shallow bowl with flaring sides on a shallow ring foot. On the interior are three stippled cartouches (possibly added later) worked by diamond point, bearing Arabic inscriptions which can be rendered 'The Divine Decree is God's,' 'Gratitude to God,' and 'Authority is God's.' Four-character reign mark 'Qianlong nian zhi' incised in double square on base.

For another piece, in the Victoria and Albert Museum, with an Islamic inscription, see Warren, 'Later Chinese Glass,' fig. 25.

15 Vase
carved transparent amber
h 12.4 cm (4⅞ in)
Qianlong mark and period (1736-95)

Bulbous body and short tapering neck, on short ring foot. The neck encircled by two archaic dragons with split tails, one ascending and the other descending, carved in high relief. The body wrapped in a diaper-patterned shawl tied with a sash. Air bubbles throughout. Six-character reign mark 'Da Qing Qianlong nian zhi' carved in seal script on base.

16 Water Jar
colorless opalescent ground with transparent aquamarine overlay
h 3.8 cm (1½ in)
first half 18th century

Small globular jar. Overlay relatively thick and with striations of brown, deeply carved to represent a diaper-patterned shawl tied with a sash. Shape probably salvaged from vase damaged in course of carving.

17 Vase
translucent ivory ground with blue overlay
h 17.5 cm (6⅞ in)
Qianlong mark and period (1736-95)

Around the body are two dragons among clouds. The shoulder decorated by a ring of *ruyi* lappets, and banana leaves encircle a neck capped by a ring of overlay. A band of stylized leaves is set above the flaring base, which is formed of overlay and bears a pontil mark. The four incised characters of the reign mark 'Qianlong nian zhi' are placed along the periphery of the base as on the vase in fig. 5 of the Yang Boda essay below.

18 Covered Jar
translucent ivory with veined opaque liver overlay
h 10.2 cm (4 in), with cover
Qianlong mark and period (1736-95)

Globular jar with individually applied and carved overlays forming shallow ring with border pattern of lotus panels, and neck with border of three archaic dragons holding branches of *lingzhi* fungus. The lid is of low profile, formed entirely of the liver-colored glass and carved with an archaic dragon holding a *lingzhi* fungus. Exceptionally well-carved and well-finished, the body of medium thickness. Incised four-character reign mark 'Qianlong nian zhi' in a bold square on base.

19 Gourd-shaped Vase
clear pink-speckled ground with transparent blue overlay
h 15.5 cm (6⅛ in)
mid 18th century

Vase of double-gourd shape with short cylindrical neck and slightly splayed foot. Overlay at neck and foot, the body with individually applied and carved overlays representing sprigs of fruiting gourd. The clear ground suffused with bubbles.

Ex-collection: Professor and Mrs. P. H. Plesch.
Published: Felice Mehlman, *Phaidon Guide to Glass* (Englewood Cliffs, NJ, 1983): 46.

20 Jar
transparent amethyst ground with transparent amethyst and veined opaque green overlays
h 11.7 cm (4⅝ in)
first half 18th century

Globular jar with short neck and shallow applied ring foot. Body with individually applied and carved overlays representing archaic dragons with split tails grasping *lingzhi* fungi, along with two simulated ring-handles with *taotie* masks. Medium thick body with thick overlays. Three overlays of transparent amethyst; one archaic dragon overlay of veined green simulating malachite. Scattered air bubbles and inclusions throughout.

21 Small Vase
transparent amethyst with overlays of opaque pink and transparent light blue over white
h 14.3 cm (5⅝ in)
first half 18th century

Vase with slightly flaring neck, tapering body, slightly splayed base, and shallow ring foot. Individually applied overlays carved to represent pine, bamboo, prunus with butterflies, bats, peaches. Scattered air bubbles.

22 Incense Burner
transparent green (with partial inner casing in white) with
multicolor overlays
h 10.2 cm (4 in), with cover
first half 18th century

Ding-shaped incense burner with three cabriole feet. Body with
individually applied and carved overlays representing three archaic dragons with bifurcated tails among *lingzhi* fungi. Thick
body of transparent green streaked with black; relatively deep
overlays of mingled transparent red, opaque white, brown, and
yellow. Carved wooden cover with cloisonné knob.

23 Jar
transparent green with opaque veined tan overlay
h 9.8 cm (3⅞ in)
second half 18th century

Jar with narrow flaring mouth, on a ring foot formed of overlay.
Deeply overlaid with variegated glass (opaque tan with striations
of transparent amber) simulating agate, deeply carved in pattern
of intertwining archaic dragons. Thick body suffused with small
air bubbles.

24 Large Vase
snowflake white with transparent red overlay
h 28.6 cm (11¼ in)
second half 18th century

The globular body surmounted by a tall cylindrical neck set off at top by a collar of banana leaves and at bottom by lotus panels. Applied pedestal base. The thick and deeply carved overlay represents a boatman, woodcutter, farmer and scholar in a landscape with pavilions.

25 Vase
opaque white with opaque red overlay
h 18.1 cm (7⅛ in)
late 18th - early 19th century

Vase with gently tapering body, flared mouth and short ring foot. Body decorated with scrolling lotus blossoms, bordered at shoulder and base with lotus panels, and a border of stylized banana leaves at mouth. Thick body with overlay of medium thickness.

Published: Felice Mehlman, 'Chinese Glass,' *Antique Collector*, vol. 51, no. 8 (August 1980): 72.

26 Vase
opaque 'mutton-fat' white with overlays of red and amber-yellow
h 19 cm (7⅜ in)
second half 18th century

Vase with cylindrical neck and flaring ring foot. Body and neck with individually applied and carved overlays representing archaic dragons with split tails chasing a flaming pearl. Body of medium thickness, opalescent with striations. Scattered bubbles.

Two similar vases, illustrated in Gunhild Gabbert, *Chinesisches Glas*, (Museum für Kunsthandwerk, Frankfurt, 1980), nos. 624, 625, are dated by the author into the 19th century.

27 Vase
opaque 'mutton-fat' white with transparent red overlay
h 19.1 cm (7½ in)
Qianlong mark and period (1736-95)

Vase with gently tapering body, cylindrical neck and slightly recessed base formed of overlay. Body decorated with intertwining dragons pursuing a flaming pearl; lower border of waves and rocks (*shoushan fuhai*, longevity mountain, prosperity sea), upper border of *ruyi* lappets, and silkworms and bosses encircling neck capped with ring of overlay. Medium thickness, well-finished interior. Superb carving rich variation in relief. Base drilled for use as lamp; resulting cracks. Four-character reign mark 'Qianlong nian zhi' incised in double square on base.

28 Pair of Covered Jars
yellow snowflake with opaque red overlay
h 14.6 cm (5¾ in), with cover
Qianlong mark and probably period

Globular jars with gently tapering body and four stepped feet. Body decorated in pattern of frolicking Buddhist lions in four roundels with upper border of *ruyi* lappets and geometric border below. Lid with frolicking lions and brocaded balls. Thick body with thick overlay. Base with incised four-character reign mark 'Qianlong nian zhi' in single square.

For a red-on-yellow covered jar of similar shape in the Victoria and Albert Museum, see Warren, 'Later Chinese Glass,' fig. 43. A red-on-yellow vase with a similar stepped foot is illustrated in Harvey Stupler, 'Antiques: The Art of Peking Glass,' *Architectural Digest* (March 1982): 110.

29 Vase
yellow snowflake with opaque red overlay
h 22.9 cm (9 in)
Qianlong mark and probably period

Vase with tapering neck and splayed ring foot. Overlay at neck carved to represent archaic dragons; geometric interlace of stylized dragons on body. A border of *ruyi* lappets circles the waist. Base with incised four-character reign mark 'Qianlong nian zhi' in seal script.

30 Cup
opaque white with transparent blue overlay
h 7.3 cm (2⅞ in)
first half 19th century

Cup on shallow ring foot, the overlay crisply carved with scene of birds and flowering prunus and camellias. Rim encircled with ring of overlay. Relatively thick-walled body.

31 Large Four-sided Vase
opaque white with blue overlay
h 26 cm (10¼ in)
mid 19th century

Four-sided vase with gently tapering body, cylindrical neck and shallow square foot. Four reserve panels on body with seasonal flowers: prunus, peony, lotus and camellia. Border of lotus panels at shoulder and stylized banana leaf pattern at neck. Thick body.

32 Vase
translucent white with blue overlay
h 21.9 cm (8⅝ in)
first half 19th century
Vase with tall cylindrical neck and flaring ring foot. Exterior carved with pine, blossoming prunus and lily growing from a ground of stylized rocks. Upper border of *ruyi* lappets and bosses. Body and well-carved overlay of varying thickness.

Published: Mehlman, 'Chinese Glass,' 72.

33 Stemmed Cup
translucent white with blue overlay
h 12 cm (4¾ in)
mid 19th century

Ovoid bowl with wide mouth and narrow stem. Pedestal foot raised on a band of *ruyi* lappets. Exceptionally thin opalescent white body, the overlay carved in a pattern of intertwining lotus blossoms on the body, with border of stylized *ruyi* fungus.

34 Bowl
translucent white with blue overlay
d 14.9 cm (5⅞ in)
Qianlong mark but 19th century

Bowl with rounded sides, everted lip and ring foot. Outer surface carved with pattern of three *shou* (longevity) medallions encircled by five bats and interspersed with three tassled coins suspended by bats. Body of medium thickness, the interior recessed into ring foot. Base incised with six-character reign mark 'Da Qing Qianlong nian zhi' in seal-script in square.

35 Vase
opaque blue-green imitating celadon
h 21 cm (8¼ in)
Qianlong mark and period (1736-95)

Globular body with tall cylindrical neck and flaring ring foot. Surface well polished, revealing minute black inclusions. Base with incised four-character reign mark 'Qianlong nian zhi' in double square.

For a similar opaque turquoise vase with a Yongzheng mark in the British Museum, see D. B. Harden, *Masterpieces of Glass* (London, 1968), fig. 169.

36 Vase
translucent 'mutton-fat' white
h 24.1 cm (9½ in)
Qianlong mark but first half 19th century

Pear-shaped vase with tall cylindrical neck and shallow ring foot. Thick-walled opalescent body. Incised six-character reign mark 'Da Qing Qianlong nian zhi' on base in seal-script.

37 Bowl
opaque yellow
d 15.9 cm (6¼ in)
Qianlong mark and period (1736-95)

Bowl with slightly everted rim and ring foot. Incised and gilded six-character mark 'Da Qing Qianlong nian zhi' incised in seal-script on base.

38 Pair of Vases
translucent yellow
h 22 cm (8⅝ in)
Qianlong mark and period (1736-95)

The shoulder and part of the body carved in relief with geometric interlace of stylized dragons. Poem by the Qianlong emperor, apparently written during one of his Southern Inspection Tours, incised and gilded in reserve panels. Gilded six-character seal-script reign mark 'Da Qing Qianlong nian zhi' incised on slightly recessed base.

Published: Mehlman, *Phaidon Guide to Glass:* 14.

39 Large Vase
opaque yellow
h 25.7 cm (10⅛ in)
Qianlong mark and period (1736-95)

Globular body with tall cylindrical neck and ring foot. Inscriptions carved on three cartouches on body (the Lanting – Orchid Pavilion – preface, one of the most revered poetic compositions of Chinese literature and a standard text for calligraphy; for translation, see Monica and T. C. Lai, *Rhapsodic Essays from the Chinese*, Hong Kong, 1979), and on two scroll-shaped panels on neck (the Qianlong emperor's brief introduction to the preface). Six-character seal-script reign mark 'Da Qing Qianlong nian zhi' incised on base.

For another yellow vase with a long Qianlong inscription, see Warren, 'Later Chinese Glass,' figs. 36a, 36b.

40 Vase
opaque orange and yellow imitating realgar
h 23.5 cm (9¼ in)
Qianlong mark and period (1736-95)

Globular body with tall cylindrical neck. Slightly recessed base incised with four-character reign mark 'Qianlong nian zhi' in double square.

Two other examples of simulated realgar, a waste jar and a bowl, are in the Museum of Far Eastern Antiquities, Stockholm, formerly Carl Kempe collection.

41 Covered Incense Burner
opaque pink and white imitating coral
h 9.8 cm (3⅞ in), with cover
late 19th century

Ding-shaped incense burner with three short, curved feet. Body carved with two *taotie* masks, with incised key-fret border on raised band at rim, and set with two dragon-head handles. The cover carved with two swirling dragons whose heads meet upright at center to form the knob. Pores and pinholes on the surface in keeping with the imitation of coral.

42 Pair of Vases
opaque red imitating carnelian
h 22.5 cm (8⅞ in)
late 19th century

Bulbous octagonal body, flared neck with everted rim, and broad bases lightly countersunk. The pair carved with mirror-image decoration of Eight Taoist Immortals in reserve panels.

43 Mallet-Shaped Vase
opaque turquoise
h 17.8 cm (7 in)
Jiaqing mark and period (1796-1820)

Mallet-shaped vase with projecting ring at neck and slightly recessed base incised with four-character reign mark 'Jiaqing nian zhi' in double square.

44 Vase
opaque turquoise with snowflake yellow overlay
h 18.1 cm (7⅛ in)
late 18th - early 19th century

Vase with gently tapering body, flared mouth and ring foot. Body decorated with scene of deer and cranes among pines and rocks, beneath moon and clouds; *lingzhi* fungi scattered throughout.

45 Lobed Narcissus Bowl
opaque turquoise
20 × 14 cm (7⅞ × 5½ in)
Qianlong mark and period (1736-95)

Four-lobed narcissus bowl with four raised foot-pads on a base incised with four-character reign mark 'Qianlong nian zhi' in double square.

For a similar piece in the Tokyo National Museum, see Suntory Museum of Art, *Kenryū garasu to āru nūvō* (Tokyo, 1983), no. 112.

46 Pair of Large Vases
opaque turquoise
h 28.9 cm (11⅜ in)
second half 18th century

Gu-shaped vase with trumpet mouth, central swelling and flared base. Carved in relief with border of *ruyi* lappets on rim, lotus scrolls between borders of stiff banana leaves on body, and lotus panels at foot.

Published: Melhman, *Phaidon Guide to Glass*: 47.

47 Large Bowl
opaque turquoise
d 28 cm (11 in)
Qianlong mark and period (1736-95)

Large heavy-walled bowl with steep sides and everted rim, the interior deeply recessed into ring foot. Boldly carved on exterior with a broad frieze of flowering lotus. Base with incised four-character reign mark 'Qianlong nian zhi' in bold square.

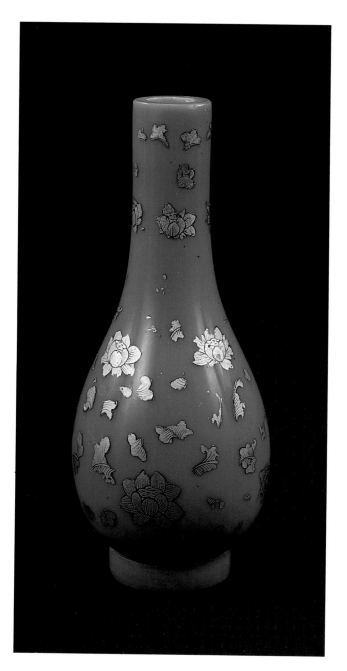

48 Vase
opaque blue cased over a lighter blue and decorated with gold
h 18.4 cm (7¼ in)
Qianlong mark and period (1736-95)

Pear-shaped body with slender cylindrical neck, on a ring foot. Decoration, partly worn, in gold applied over red mastic, with details picked out in black, representing lotus flowers and scattered leaves. Base painted in gold with four-character reign mark 'Qianlong nian zhi.'

49 Vase
opaque white, carved and enameled
h 13 cm (5½ in)
guyuexuan mark, late 18th - early 19th century

Vase with globular body, slightly tapering cylindrical neck, and ring foot. Body is carved with four reserve panels, each with scenes of birds and flowers in relief and painted in *famille rose* enamels: a quail on a rock beneath a spray of millet; a phoenix among peonies under a cloud-obscured sun; a deer under a pine with a bat and *lingzhi* fungi; and a crane with pine and peonies. Traces of 'guyuexuan' mark on base.

Published: Hugh Moss, 'Enamelled Glass Wares of the Ku Yüeh Hsüan Type,' *Journal of the International Chinese Snuff Bottle Society*, vol. 10, no. 2 (June 1978), fig. 6.

50 Small Vase
opaque white with enamels
h 10.2 cm (4 in)
guyuexuan mark, late 18th - early 19th century

Globular body with slightly flaring neck, enamelled in *famille rose* colors with a long-tailed phoenix beside peony sprays on a grassy plateau. The neck draped with tassles suspended from *ruyi* lappets beneath key-fret band. 'Guyuexuan' mark in faint red enamel on base.

Similar piece illustrated in Moss, 'Enamelled Glass Wares,' fig. 8.

51 Pair of Vases
transparent red
h 22.5 cm (8⅞ in)
mid 19th century

Vases with slightly tapering body, flared mouth and shallow ring foot. Bodies carved with flowers and dragonflies.

52 Guanyin
transparent blue
h 27.3 cm (10⅜ in)
second half 19th century

Molded figure of the bodhisattva Guanyin, the vertical join of the mold smoothly finished.

A virtually identical Guanyin, possibly from the same mold but in amber-colored glass, is in the British Museum Collection; see Harold Newman, *Illustrated Dictionary of Glass* (London, 1977): 175.

53 Octagonal Vase
transparent green
h 14 cm (5½ in)
Daoguang mark and period (1821-50)

Octagonal pear-shaped vase with flaring ring foot. Thin body, very few air bubbles. Base with incised four-character reign mark 'Daoguang nian zhi' in single square.

Published: Mehlman, *Phaidon Guide to Glass*: 49.

54 Mallet Vase
carved dark transparent blue cased over layers of light and dark blue
h 19.7 cm (7¾ in)
first half 19th century

Vase with tall cylindrical neck and slightly recessed base. The neck carved with fruited branches, the body with landscape scene with scholar, boatmen, and pavilion.

55 Large Foliate Dish
transparent blue
d 34 cm (13⅜ in)
second half 19th century

Large dish molded and carved as a lotus blossom, the petals concave on the interior and convex on the exterior (in the manner of Yuan and Ming celadon designs) and enclosed within a scalloped rim. Interior of bowl recessed into ring foot. 'Chicken skin' pores along lower ridges and on base.

For a similar piece, see Warren, 'Later Chinese Glass,' fig. 23.

56 Bowl
transparent amethyst
d 20.3 cm (8 in)
mid 19th century

Bowl with everted rim, the interior deeply recessed into ring foot.

57 Pair of Shallow Bowls
transparent red
d 17.1 cm (6¾ in)
Qianlong mark but probably mid 19th century

Shallow bowls with ring foot. The color may result from ruby red flashing or casing over clear glass. Scattered pinpoint bubbles. The base incised with four-character reign mark 'Qianlong nian zhi' in seal script in bold square.

58 Incense Burner
transparent yellow with partial inner casing of translucent yellow
h 8.9 cm (3½ in)
Qianlong mark and period (1736-95)

Round *ding*-shaped incense burner with three conical feet, the
body with scattered bubbles and small inclusions. Four-character
reign mark 'Qianlong nian zhi' incised in double square on base.

59 Large Jar
carved opaque yellow
h 24.4 cm (9⅝ in)
second half 19th century

Large ovoid jar with slightly recessed base, carved in archaistic
pattern of squared spirals with dragon heads and upper border of
stylized banana leaves.

60 Small Vase
opaque mustard yellow
h 13 cm (5⅛ in)
first half 19th century

Meiping-shaped vase with short and flared neck above gently slop-
ing shoulders, on a recessed base. The glass darkens around the
shoulders, and the polished surface reveals several small bubbles.

61 Covered Jar
opaque white with opaque blue overlay
h 17.8 cm (7 in), with cover
19th century

Ovoid jar with sides tapering to a flat base; fitted lid surmounted
by a flaring knob. Jar and lid entirely cased in blue then carved in
horizontally arranged facets, each slightly concave and revealing
an eye of white.

62 Small Gourd-shaped Bottle
opaque 'mutton fat' white with transparent red overlay
h 8.6 cm (3⅜ in)
second half 18th century

Small vase of double-gourd shape on three gourd-shaped feet
formed of overlay. Finely carved overlay representing twining
vines with gourds.

For a smaller bottle of similar type, see Shen Zhiyu, *The Shanghai
Museum of Art* (New York, 1981), pl. 230.

63 Pair of Vases
opaque white with red overlay
h 20.8 cm (8¼ in)
second half 19th century

Pair of pear-shaped vases with gently widening neck and rim
thickened by overlay. Slightly flaring ring foot. Transparent raspberry red overlay carved in identical scenes of three ladies in a
garden, one playing a musical instrument, one dancing, one serv-
ing tea. Garden setting with rocks, pawlonia tree, butterfly, *lingzhi*
fungus and chrysanthemum. Body of medium weight, well-
carved overlay of varying depth.

64 Bowl
opaque white with red overlay
d 16.4 cm (6⅜ in)
second half 19th century

Bowl with gently flaring sides and everted rim, the interior
recessed into ring foot. Exterior overlay carved with scene of three
scholars, one with boy servant, in a landscape setting of pavilions,
rocks and pine trees, with distant mountains. Raspberry red overlay of varying depth on a relatively thick ground.

65 Brush Pot
opaque white with multicolor overlays
h 10.8 cm (4¼ in)
late 19th century

Slender cylindrical brush pot with shallow ring foot of blue overlay. Individually applied overlays in seven colors (blue, light blue,
red, yellow, pink, beeswax and green) representing auspicious
emblems: fan, musical instrument, vase with flowers, incense
burner, scroll inscribed 'da ji' (great good luck), pair of scrolls,
weiqi board, bat, peaches, and musical stone.

66 Pair of Bowls
carved opaque green imitating jade or celadon
d 16.2 cm (6¼ in)
first half 19th century

Bowls with gently flaring sides and rim, the interior recessed into
ring foot. Outer surface carved with scene of waterfowl and
lotuses springing from stylized waves. Opposite matching pair.

For a bowl of similar color and decoration in the Suntory Museum
of Art, Tokyo, see *Kenryū garasu*, fig. 127.

67 Pair of Vases
carved opaque yellow
h 21.6 cm (8½ in)
second half 19th century

Meiping-shaped vases with tapering body and flared base and
mouth, on shallow ring foot. Bodies of medium thickness carved
with opposite matching scenes of ladies in a garden with pine,
willow, magnolia and prunus.

68 Pair of Narcissus Bowls
translucent white with green overlay
22.1 × 18 cm (8¾ × 7⅛ in)
late 19th century

Pair of narcissus bowls, each with four-lobed rim, the lobes con-
tinuing down the body to the shallow oval ring foot. Transparent
green overlay carved with opposite matching landscapes. One
side with a boy on a water buffalo lowering himself to pick up a
hat. The other, a sage with a staff standing on a bridge beneath
gnarled branches, the scene set within mountains with pines,
willows, and pavilions.

69 Vase
carved opaque yellow
h 18.1 cm (7⅛ in)
second half 19th century

Vase with tapering body, flaring rim, and slightly recessed base.
Outer surface carved in high relief with highly sculptural motifs
of tiger and dragon above waves and against incised cloud pattern. Body of medium thickness.

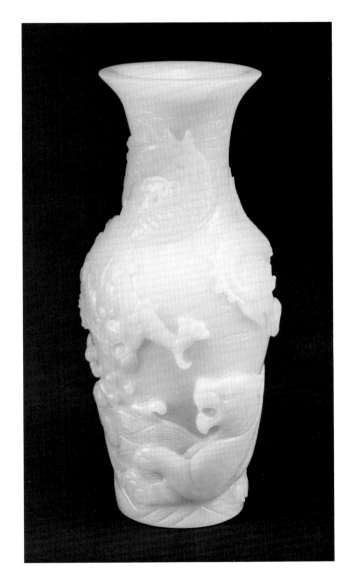

70 Bell
carved opaque white
h 9.2 cm (3⅝ in)
late 19th century

Bell carved with stylized animal heads at top, drilled for suspension. Body with incised decoration of two *ruyi* and two circles between double rings.

71 Bowl
carved opaque white
d 16.6 cm (6½ in)
second half 19th century

Bowl with flaring sides and everted rim, the interior sharply recessed into ring foot. Exterior carved with birds and flowering prunus. Walls of medium thickness.

72 Covered Tea Bowl
opaque white
d 10.5 cm (4⅛ in)
second half 19th century

Bowl with flaring sides and slightly everted rim, on flared ring foot. Bowl and cover relatively thin with heavier bases.

73 Pair of Bowls
opaque pink
d 16.3 cm (6⅜ in)
second half 19th century

Pair of bowls with slightly everted rim and ring foot, the exterior
cut with three registers of facets.

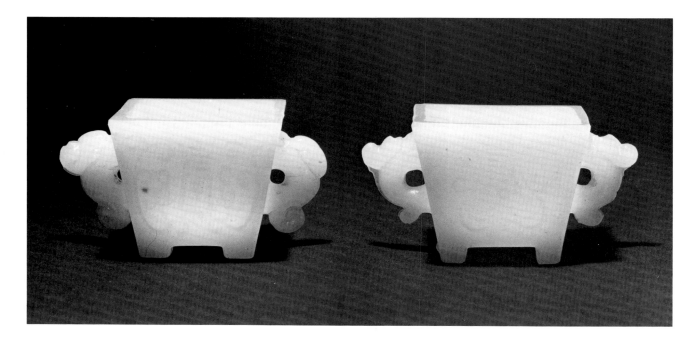

74 Two Cups
translucent greenish white imitating jade
h 4.9 cm (1⅞ in)
late 17th - early 18th century

Two molded cups, each of tapering squared form with corner
bracket feet and dragon handles, the scrolling animals single-
horned and short tailed. One cup decorated on each side in low,
linear relief with a *shou* (longevity) character in a stylized mask;
the other with a similar *shou* character and two stylized birds.
Prominent mold marks.

Two cups of the same type and size are in the Bishop W. C. White
Collection in the Royal Ontario Museum, Toronto, illustrated in
Doris Dohrenwend, 'Glass in China: A Review Based on the
Collection of the Royal Ontario Museum,' *Oriental Art* 26 (1980-81),
p. 439, fig. 31, where a Kangxi date is suggested. A related example in jade is illustrated in James C. Y. Watt, *Chinese Jades from Han
to Ch'ing* (The Asia Society, New York, 1980), no. 141.

76 Archer's Ring
carved transparent blue
d 3.4 cm (1⅜ in)
19th century

Cylindrical archer's thumb ring, slightly tapering. Exterior carved with geometric interlace of stylized dragons reviving Late Zhou decorative patterns.

75 Pair of Scroll or Paper Weights
engraved transparent blue
l 13 cm (5⅛ in)
19th century

Elongated oblongs, the curved upper surface wheel-engraved with flowering peonies bordered by endless-knot pattern.

77 Box for Seal Pigment
translucent deep purple
d 4.9 cm (1⅞ in)
19th century

Flat, round box with slightly recessed base, probably for vermilion seal pigment.

78 Snuff Bottle
clear glass, interior painted
h 7.3 cm (2⅞ in), with stopper
dated 1905 and signed Ma Shaoxuan

The interior abraded and painted. One side with lotus flowers and
a bird, the brief inscription indicating that this was a presentation
bottle to be offered following success in the civil service examina-
tions. The other side with a poem, and signed by the painter Ma
Shaoxuan (active 1895-1923).

For discussion of Ma Shaoxuan's activity, see Schuyler Cammann,
'Chinese Inside-painted Snuff Bottles and Their Makers,' *Harvard
Journal of Asiatic Studies*, vol. 20, nos. 1-2 (June 1957): 295-326.
Several of his works are illustrated in *Snuff Bottles of the Ch'ing
Dynasty* (Hong Kong Museum of Art), 1978.

79 Snuff Bottle
opaque white with painted enamel
h 6.8 cm (2⅝ in) , with stopper
Qianlong mark but first half 19th century

Flattened ovoid snuff bottle of the *guyuexuan* type. Enamelled decoration in blue, pink, red, lemon-yellow, aubergine, and green, representing a gathering at a river bank. The base with red-enamelled reign mark 'Qianlong nian zhi' in seal-script.

80 Large Snuff Bottle
snowflake white with deep red overlay
h 10.5 cm (4⅛ in), with stopper
late 19th century

Flat, round snuff bottle with oval foot in overlay. Roundels on either side carved in overlay: tiger and bat on one side, dragon in waves on the other. Simulated ring handles with *taotie* masks. Neck with a border of stylized leaves. Deep overlay on a relatively heavy body.

81 Snuff Bottle
snowflake white with transparent blue overlay
h 6.4 cm (2½ in), with stopper
late 18th century

Flat, round bottle with oval foot in overlay. Shallow overlay well-carved with scene of figures in a landscape: a scholar in a pavilion, a herdsman with buffalo, a fisherman and a wood gatherer.

82 Toggle
translucent greenish white imitating jade
h 5.8 cm (2⅜ in)
19th century

Lamp-worked toggle in the shape of a Buddha-hand fruit or finger citron, drilled for suspension.

83 Pendant
yellow ice with transparent red overlay, imitating hornbill
3.2 × 4.5 cm (1¼ × 1¾ in)
18th century

Front with red overlay carved to represent an archaic dragon, back with same motif carved in yellow ground. Drilled for use as a pendant or toggle.

84 Bracelet
translucent greenish white imitating jade
d 8.8 cm (3½ in)
19th - 20th century

Large annular bracelet, a pigmented area suggesting veins of color in jade.

85 Belt Buckle
opaque white imitating 'mutton-fat' jade
3.6 × 5.2 cm (1⅜ × 2 in) exclusive of mounting
18th century

Belt buckle in archaistic style carved in shallow relief with *shou* (longevity) character set between two bats and two geometric interlaces of stylized dragons. Gilt bronze mounting.

86 Toggle
translucent white imitating 'mutton-fat' jade
3.7 × 5.7 cm (1½ × 2¼ in)
19th century

Plaque pierced, molded, and carved on both sides, representing climbing cat.

87 Toggle
opaque white imitating 'mutton-fat' jade
4.1 × 6.1 cm (1⅝ × 2⅜ in)
19th century

Molded and carved plaque, the upper portion pierced with archaic dragon, the plaque carved on both sides with lotus decoration.

88 Toggle
translucent greenish white imitating jade
h 4.1 cm (1⅝ in)
19th century

Lamp-worked pendant in the shape of a Buddha-hand fruit or finger citron, with loop for suspension.

89 Toggle
opaque white imitating 'mutton-fat' jade
h 5.4 cm (2⅛ in)
late 19th century

Toggle molded and carved in the shape of a small boy.

90 Ring
translucent white imitating 'mutton-fat' jade
d 3.5 cm (1⅜ in)
19th - 20th century

Annular ring, possibly intended as a ring handle.

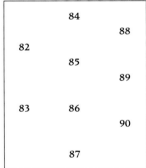

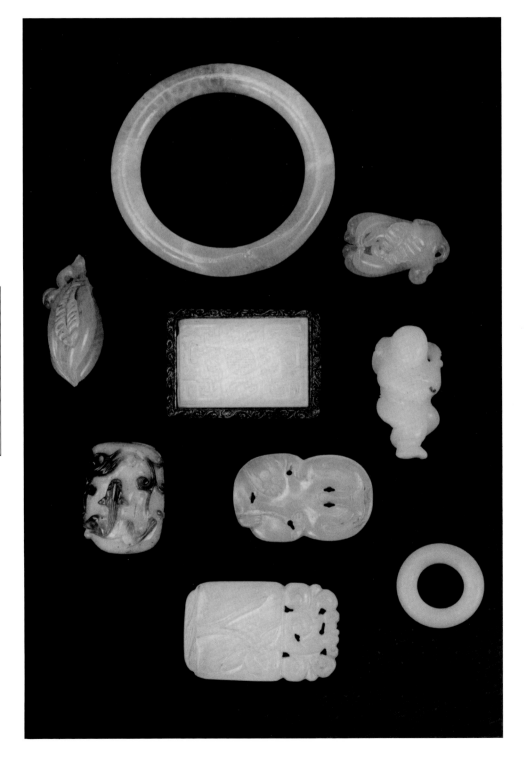

91 String of Beads
various colors
d 1 to 1.9 cm (⅜ to ¾ in)
18th century

The small opaque yellow beads are ground and polished. The thirteen larger round and oval beads are of various opaque ground colors laced with multi-colored canes. The latter are ground but not polished.

92 Opium Lamp
clear ground, the bulb with transparent red overlay
h 15.9 cm (6¼ in)
second half 19th century

The lamp consists of a base with chimney, a stem and a bulb with cover. Openwork carving on base with bats alternating with coins, the foot of openwork prunus blossoms alternating with *ruyi* heads. Bulb with red overlay carved to represent bats.

For a nineteenth-century photograph of a man using this type of lamp, see Burton F. Beers, *China in Old Photographs*, 1860-1910 (Milton, MA, 1978), fig. 55. For similar opium lamps with more conventional metal bases, see Patrick Maveety, *Opium: Pipes, Prints, and Paraphernalia* (Stanford University Museum of Art, 1979), nos. 89 and 91.

Chronology of the Qing Dynasty

Shunzhi	1644-1661
Kangxi	1662-1722
Yongzheng	1723-1735
Qianlong	1736-1795
Jiaqing	1796-1820
Daoguang	1821-1850
Xianfeng	1851-1861
Tongzhi	1862-1874
Guangxu	1875-1908
Xuantong	1909-1911

Yang Boda, Vice-director
Palace Museum, Beijing

A Brief Account of Qing Dynasty Glass

Glassmaking has a long history in China. The Chinese were making glass as early as the Western Zhou dynasty (eleventh century-771 BC), according to recent excavations.[1] With improvements in production techniques, glassmaking progressed from simple ornaments like round and tubular beads to ritual and everyday utensils, imitation gems, and burial articles. The color of glass developed from a monochromatic light blue to a range of greens, blues, purples, and blacks, and from opaque to translucent and transparent.

Glass was first manufactured in Shenxi Province. From there, its manufacture expanded eastward to Henan and Shandong, southward to Hubei, Hunan, Guangdong, and Guangxi, and gradually through all of China. Chemical analysis indicates that ancient Chinese glass, which is distinguished from Western glass by its bright colors and unique shapes, belonged to the low-firing lead-barium group. Later, with the increase of trade and cultural exchange between East and West, European glass entered China by land and by sea, and Western merchants and missionaries familiar with glassmaking brought new techniques into China. Thus by the Qing dynasty (1644-1911), the Chinese glassmaking tradition, which had evolved distinctive characteristics over the course of three millenia, was further enhanced through its openness to foreign technology.[2]

Characteristics

Great improvements in the manufacture of glass in the Ming dynasty (1368-1643) laid the foundation for progress in the Qing period. One early Qing book, *Yanshan zaji* (Mt. Yan miscellany) by Sun Tingquan, gives evidence that glassmaking at Yanshenzhen in Boshan county had reached a significant level during the Ming dynasty.[3] However, during the thirteenth and fourteenth year of Chongzheng (1640-41), a drought hit the area north of the Yangtze River. Ninety percent of the glassmakers from Boshan died and the industry was seriously damaged. Not until early in the reign of Kangxi (1662-1722) did glass manufacture begin to flourish again at Yanshenzhen.

Towards the end of the Ming dynasty, trade ships from Western European countries sailed the thousands of miles around the Cape of Good Hope, through the Indian Ocean, and into the South and the East China Sea, entering the ports of Guangzhou (Canton), Zhangzhou (Amoy harbor), Quanzhou, and Ningbo to sell their merchandise.[4] Trade by sea was prohibited in the early Qing dynasty until the reign of Kangxi, when Guangzhou became the major port through which the Chinese had contact with the Western countries. Many novel and unusual articles, such as clocks and watches, gems, coral, enamel wares, and glass, were imported into China. This merchandise held great appeal for the emperor, aristocracy, and high ranking officials. Western production techniques also took root in Guangzhou, which became a center for trade and for the Chinese manufacture of clocks, watches, enamels, and glass.

Originally published as 'Qingdai boli gaishu' (Survey of Qing Period Glass), *Gugong Bowuyuan yuankan* (1983, no. 4): 3-17. Translation by Wynette Yao. Edited and adapted by Donald Rabiner.

Pieces illustrated in this essay are in the collection of the Palace Museum.

The respect of the Qing court for the missionaries was based on their expertise in such subjects as astronomy, mathematics, physics, surveying, mechanics, painting, and architecture. Various bureaus within the court absorbed missionaries with these specialties, providing large material rewards and excellent working conditions to promote the full exercise of their talents. Those who had knowledge of glassmaking participated directly in the imperial glass workshop, furthering the introduction of Western techniques into China and improving traditional Chinese glassmaking.

With all these advantages, Qing glass production flourished, developing different characteristics from that of preceding dynasties. The imperial glass workshop brought together glassmakers from Yanshenzhen and Guangdong, resulting in exchange of information among glassmakers from the north and the south. Traditional techniques were improved and new kinds of glass were created, the outstanding ones being *tao liao* (overlay) and *jian tao* (multiple overlay). Moreover, the Chinese were able to absorb European glassmaking techniques from the missionaries. Many new styles and shapes as well as new kinds of glass, such as aventurine glass, were introduced in this period of Chinese glassmaking.

Qing glass production was also marked by enthusiastic support from the emperor, princes, and high officials. From the time Kangxi ordered the establishment of an imperial glass workshop, the manufacture of glass almost never ceased. In a period spanning some two hundred years, the imperial workshop produced a large quantity of glass, including ritual utensils, articles of display, writing implements, a variety of ornaments, and snuff bottles. These items were used as gifts for imperial relatives, high officials, foreign rulers, and their ambassadors.

In the Kangxi period, glass imitations of gems became increasingly refined, and lenses of black glass were used for the eyes of the golden dragons embroidered on court costumes. During the Yongzheng reign (1723-35), glass was used in place of gems for official insignia. A third-class officer would use clear blue glass in place of sapphire in the top-knot of his hat; a fourth-class officer, opaque blue glass for lapis lazuli; a fifth-class officer, clear glass in place of rock crystal; and a sixth-class officer, opaque white glass instead of mother-of-pearl.[5] By the late Qing dynasty, the substitution of glass for gems was even more common.

The imperialist invasion of China during the Opium Wars of the nineteenth century brought economic exploitation and political suppression. As the economy collapsed, and agricultural and industrial production fell, the manufacture of glass gradually declined. Nevertheless, shortly before its collapse in 1911 the Qing government established a government-owned glass company and hired foreign technicians in a final effort to produce glass on a large scale.

The Distribution of Manufacturing Sites

China boasts an abundance of the natural materials used in making glass, and the history of Chinese glassmaking is long and illustrious. Nonetheless, little is known about where and when the making of glass began in China. Records from the earliest period of glass production, the Western Zhou dynasty, provide us with no information about manufacturing sites, and only scattered references from the Sui (581- 618) through the Song (960-1279) dynasties document glass production in such cities as Changan and Suzhou.[6] In the Ming dynasty, glass was manufactured in Yanshenzhen in Shandong Province and in the Qi region north of the Huai River.[7] In the Qing dynasty, glass manufacturing was limited to only a few sites, which are discussed below.

Boshan County
The administrative seat of Boshan county was Yanshenzhen, located one hundred and eighty kilometers southwest of Yidu in the Tai mountains. As land for cultivation was

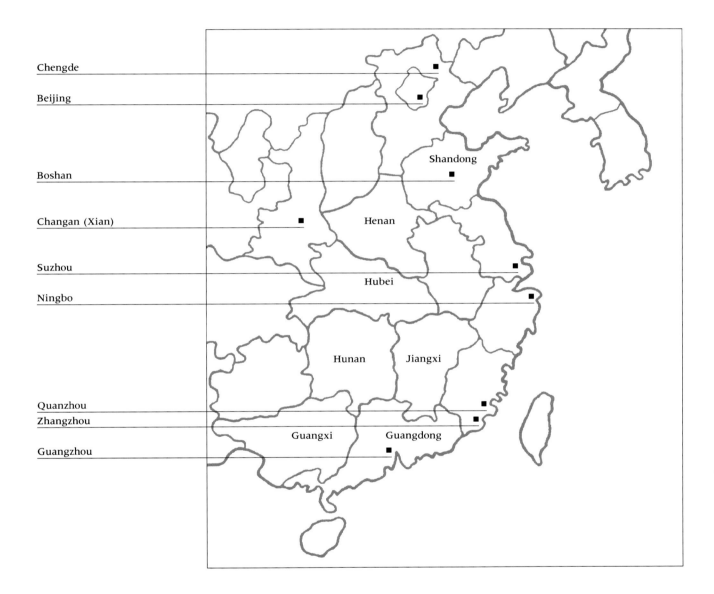

Chengde

Beijing

Boshan

Changan (Xian)

Suzhou

Ningbo

Quanzhou
Zhangzhou

Guangzhou

Shandong

Henan

Hubei

Hunan   Jiangxi

Guangxi   Guangdong

scarce in this mountainous terrain, most of the residents were engaged in coal-mining, smelting, and the manufacture of pottery and glass. Natural resources were abundant, and all the material and technical conditions necessary for the development of glassmaking were present.[8]

Unfortunately, there is no way to determine when glassmaking began at Yanshenzhen. From the records of the Sun family,[9] excavations of furnaces,[10] and recovered artifacts,[11] we can ascertain that at the latest, glassmaking had begun by the third year of the Hongwu reign (1370). Extending the date back to the Yuan dynasty (1279-1368) seems justifiable. This is still a conservative estimate, and more precise dating awaits further investigation.

Glass made at Yanshenzhen during the Ming dynasty was, according to a sixteenth-century text, 'clear, smooth and lovely.'[12] Natural resources needed in glassmaking, such as feldspar, fluorite, quartz, saltpeter, copper, iron, and lead, could all be found in Boshan and the surrounding mountains, so their transportation presented no problem. Blue window blinds were the most highly prized items produced in the Qing dynasty, while other products included pendants, decorated lanterns, screens, boxes, *weiqi* pieces, wind chimes, rosary beads, lids for teapots, lampshades, fish-shaped bottles, gourd-shaped vases, water-droppers, mirrors, and musical instruments. According to Sun Tingquan of the early Qing dynasty, such glass products were 'luxury articles,' and these were marketed 'north to Yenan, south to Baiyue, east to Korea, west beyond the Yellow River.'[13] During the Qianlong reign, glass shops concentrated on Xiye Street. By the late nineteenth century, seventy percent of the local households, including women and children, were working in the glassmaking industry. Some three hundred and fifty tons of glass products were shipped from the town annually.[14]

Guangzhou

Guangzhou (Canton), China's southern gateway to the Middle East and Europe, was a major port as early as the Tang dynasty. A thriving center of commercial exchange, through which Islamic and European glass and Western glassmaking techniques entered China, Guangzhou became an important center for glass production during the Qing dynasty.

Attitudes towards foreign glass varied during Guangzhou's long history of importing glass. Gao Lian of the late Ming recorded the shapes and colors of the glass that passed through Guangzhou, and his evaluations reflect the lack of interest of scholars and officials of the time in the products of the 'barbaric islanders.' Products like bottles, small wine glasses, tall jars, dishes, and tall stem glasses of 'twined white silk, duck green, sky blue, and yellow rim' were considered 'objects beneath the connoisseur.'[15] The Chinese of the Qing dynasty, by contrast, appreciated foreign glass very much.

Glassmaking in Guangzhou began no later than the Western Jin dynasty (265-317). The observation of Ge Hong of the Jin period that the methods for making clear glass in Guangzhou were not Chinese in origin was the first mention of glassmaking there.[16] Additional references are found in Song dynasty texts,[17] and documentation on Guangzhou glass becomes abundant in the Qing dynasty, when accomplished craftsmen from the region were sent to Beijing. 'Snuff bottles of Guangzhou glass'[18] appeared at court in the sixth year of the Yongzheng reign (1728). In the twenty-first year of Qianlong (1756), birthday offerings from the customs house in Guangzhou to the emperor included glass mirrors and covered bowls.[19] It is no longer known what materials were used in the manufacture of Guangzhou glass. Liang Tongshu (1723-1815) described Chinese glass in *Gu tongciqi kao* (A survey of ancient metalwork and porcelain) as 'brittle, breaking immediately when filled with hot water,' noting that it was manufactured in Suzhou, Guangzhou, and Qinglai in Shandong Province.[20] Derided as 'thin and brittle,' 'Guang-made' glass was called 'local' or 'native' glass in contrast to 'foreign glass,' which was praised as 'thick and crystal-like.' The poor quality of Guangzhou glass was noted by Qianlong, who on one occasion was so dissatisfied with the glass offered by the customs house in Guangzhou for his birthday festivities that he cancelled the standard reimbursement. Unfortunately, we lack information about styles and colors of Guangzhou glass.

The Imperial Glass Workshop

In the thirty-fifth year of Kangxi (1696), a glass workshop was founded on imperial order under the management of the Palace Workshop (Zaobanchu) at Yangxin Hall.[21] Lasting until the end of the Qing dynasty in 1911, the workshop produced a significant quantity of glass over the course of more than two hundred years. The craftsmen working here hailed primarily from Boshan in Shandong Province, although in the early years they came also from Guangzhou, and at times even missionaries participated. According to documents in the Qing archives, there were furnaces of every size, with the large ones used only occasionally, for making large lanterns. Small furnaces were used more frequently, and produced articles for the New Year's festivities as well as other glass ordered by the emperor. The manufacturing process required intense heat, limiting glass production to the spring, fall, and early winter. The materials were similar to those used in Boshan, and might very well have been shipped from there.

In the course of two centuries, the imperial glass workshop went from prosperity to decline, mirroring the fortunes of the Qing dynasty. Its history can be divided into four periods: the fifty years from its establishment during the Kangxi reign until the end of Yongzheng, a period of prosperity; the first twenty years of Qianlong, when it reached its peak; the second half of Qianlong to the Jiaqing era (1796-1820), a period of relative idleness; and from Daoguang (1821-50) until the fall of the Qing in 1911, the period of the workshop's final decline.

Peking Glass

Peking (Beijing) glass customarily was referred to as *liao qi*, implying 'glass made with Shandong *liao*.' The term was used among Boshan craftsmen and was adopted by merchants; in Beijing it became synonymous with 'glass.' During the period from the late Qing dynasty through the first few decades of the Republic, the material used for Peking glass was indeed from Boshan in Shandong Province. According to Bushell, Beijing merchants during the late Qing dynasty sold a glass that resembled white jade and glass tiles that were called *jing liao*, or Peking glass, but actually were made in Boshan: 'The *Ching liao* [*jing liao*], properly so called, is really made in the capital itself from glass rods and plates brought up from Po-shan [Boshan], and is far superior in design and finish, as well as in price, to the provincial production dignified by the same name.'[22] The practice of using Boshan rods and plates to make glass may have started even before late Qing dynasty,[23] and it lasted until 1949. Strictly speaking, then, Peking glass of the Qing period was not so much the product of full-scale manufacture as the result of local processing of inexpensive materials shipped to Beijing from Boshan.

It is still not clear when Beijing's commercial glass production began. Given that Beijing was the capital of the Yuan, Ming, and Qing dynasties, that centralized production was an imperial policy, and that transportation of raw materials would not have been difficult, the production of Peking glass may have begun quite early.

Suzhou Glass

The history of Suzhou glass is obscure. During the Southern Song dynasty (1127-1280), a kind of lantern made in Suzhou was called a 'Su-lantern.' An opaque glass *gui*, which is the largest glass article ever unearthed in China, was found in the late Yuan tomb of the mother of Zhang Shicheng. Whether it was made in Suzhou will be known only upon further investigation. During the Qing dynasty, 'Su-made' glass was said to be even poorer in quality than 'Guang-made.'[24]

Glassmaking Techniques

Early records provide scant information about glass manufacture in China. For example, Wang Chong of the Eastern Han wrote that Taoists melted five kinds of rocks to make multi-colored precious stones which had a luster indiscernible from that of real jade, and observed that beads that gleamed like real pearls could be made from chemicals.[25] Commenting on a reference to glass from a Central Asian state, Yan Shigu (579-645) wrote that chemicals were added to melted rocks.[26] The minerals and the manufacturing processes used are not identified. In the thirteenth century, Zhao Rugua described materials used for glass including lead, saltpeter, and gypsum,[27] our first indication that Song glass belonged to the sodium-calcium group, as opposed to the lead-barium group that characterized Chinese glass through the Han dynasty.

The *Qingzhou fuzhi* (Gazetteer of Qingzhou Prefecture), written during the Jiajing reign (1522-66) of the Ming dynasty,[28] noted that the materials used for Yanshenzhen glass were mainly feldspar ('horse-tooth stone') and fluorite, yellow lead, white lead, and copper-green. During the late Ming and early Qing dynasties, the main ingredients used at Yanshenzhen were feldspar, fluorite, quartz, saltpeter, copper, iron, and lead. These ingredients remained standard until the end of the Qing dynasty, save for a brief period during the Qianlong reign, when the glass frit consisted of feldspar, saltpeter, borax, arsenic, fluorite, and white lead in the following ratio: 47.5% feldspar, 28% saltpeter, 12.3% borax, 5.1% white lead, 5.1% arsenic, and 2% fluorite.[29] This formula, in use at the imperial glass workshop only between the fifth and the eighteenth year of Qianlong (1740-53), contains a large amount of borax and arsenic, with very little fluorite. The change appears to have been related to the activity of foreign missionaries in the glass workshop.

The most substantial record of Ming and Qing glassmaking is found in Sun Tingquan's book *Yanshan zaji* (Mt. Yan miscellany).[30] Sun was born into a family of officials who for several generations had supervised the making of glass. He became a high official at court in the early Qing dynasty, but took leave and returned to his hometown. At leisure, he was able to complete his book. In the section 'Liuli' he recorded the materials, firing temperatures, and facilities for glassmaking, as well as the types and colors of glass objects.

According to Sun Tingquan, a crucible filled with the necessary powdered ingredients was placed in a furnace. As there were no instruments with which to monitor the temperature, success depended entirely on the skill of craftsmen who could gauge the temperature from the changing colors of the flame. The flame would first appear black due to the smoke, and as the process went on, would turn red, then blue, and eventually white. 'Feldspar,' he wrote, 'was used for the body, fluorite for softening [fluxing], and quartz for luster.' The ingredients for glass of different colors were given as:

- Clear: five parts feldspar to one part fluorite and one part quartz
- Pure white: as above, with more fluorite and less feldspar and quartz

- Prunus red: three parts feldspar one part fluorite, one part quartz plus a small amount of copper and iron dust
- Blue: three parts feldspar, one part fluorite, decrease the quartz and iron, and add a small amount of copper
- Autumn yellow glass: the same ratio as for pure white glass, with the addition of some copper pebbles (ore?)
- Shadow-blue glass: the same ratio as for clear glass, plus a small amount of cobalt
- Ivory: the same as for pure white glass, with the addition of lead – the more the better
- Pure black: the same as for ivory glass; add iron
- Green: the same as for clear glass; add copper
- Gosling-yellow: the same as for green glass; decrease the amount of copper, and add a small amount of copper ore

There were two basic ways of forming glass. One was solid glass processing, which produced items like blue window blinds, pendants and *weiqi* pieces by molding, trailing, coiling, and dragging. Special techniques were used to make polychrome glass, such as sea-shell glass by mixing two different colors; agate glass, made by adding colored spots; and twined-silk glass, in which canes of color were added to the body, which was then rotated. The other basic method was hollow glass processing by free-blowing or mold-blowing to produce items like lamps, bottles, and other vessels.

Glass in the Reigns of Kangxi and Yongzheng

In the closing years of the Ming dynasty the Manchu troops swept down from the north, destabilizing the country and destroying all kinds of production, including glassmaking. Nonetheless, by the fourth year of the Kangxi reign (1665), just two decades after the founding of the Qing dynasty, glassmaking had begun to flourish again.

We can glean some information about glass production at this time from surviving records. For example, we know that in the forty-fourth year of Kangxi (1705), the Emperor arrived at Suzhou, south of the Yangtze River, and gave the official Song Luo gifts from the imperial glass workshop, including one opaque white fish bowl, two gold-flecked blue bottles, one blue dish, ten small yellow dishes, one brush pot with floral designs, one small white fish bowl, and one blue water jar with a blue base, for a total of seventeen pieces.[31] This group included three monochromes – white, yellow, and blue – as well as blue glass flecked with gold, probably in imitation of lapis lazuli. It is remarkable that the workshop was able to achieve such mastery within a decade of its founding.

Two kinds of glass confirm that techniques during the Kangxi period were more advanced than in the Ming dynasty: the gold-flecked blue glass, and *tao* or *tao liao*, cased or overlay glass. The late Qing artist and bibliophile Zhao Zhiqian (1829-84), who had examined '*tao* red' and '*tao* blue' snuff bottles made during the Kangxi years, aptly described *tao* as 'white [glass] which receives colors.'[32] Most *tao liao* had a white ground, but the category also included white glass over a colored ground and colored glass on a colored ground. Moreover, there are polychrome *tao*, known as *jian tao*, with anywhere from two to five colored overlays. *Tao liao* or *jian tao* with carving was called *kehua tao liao*, or carved overlay, while that without carving was called *su tao*, or plain overlay.

During the middle years of Kangxi's reign, the white ground could range from seashell to pearl-white in color. During the late Kangxi period, the terms lard-white, snow-white, and arrowroot-white came into use. The excellence in Kangxi glass technique is evident as well in monochromes of various hues. The poet Wang Shizhen (1634-1711) praised Kangxi glass as 'clear as crystal and red as flame,' comparable to gemstones. Zhao Zhiqian described it as 'simple, elegant, and archaic-looking, sparkling like treasures.'[33]

None of the glass mentioned in Kangxi-period documents can be identified. Glass from this period is exceedingly rare, and even the Palace Museum, Beijing, which is considered to have a major collection of glass, houses only one Kangxi piece – a hexagonal water-dropper of clear glass with a polished, faceted surface (figure 1).[34] This jar was first mold-blown, then cut and polished in the lapidary technique used for gems. On the base is an engraved mark, 'Kangxi yuzhi' (Kangxi Imperial Ware), in seal-script characters arranged in two vertical rows.

During the Kangxi period, in addition to glassmen from Yanshenzhen and missionaries from abroad, the imperial glass workshop employed craftsmen from Guangdong. In the forty-seventh year of Kangxi (1708), one Cheng Xianggui made a set of twelve carved overlay cups whose color was described as 'blue sky after rain.' A certain Zhou Jun made a set of twelve *su tao* cups of similar color in the fifty-fourth year of Kangxi (1715). In the fourth month of that year, both men returned to Guangdong, having worked at the imperial workshop for at least seven years.[35]

During the Yongzheng reign, glassmaking continued to flourish as the workshop was relocated to the Yuanming Yuan summer palace. According to the palace archives, items manufactured included grape-colored cups, globular bells, red water-droppers with drum-shaped bodies and chicken spouts, imitation-carnelian pieces, semi-opaque red cups, amber cups with carved decoration, opaque yellow beads, opaque yellow water containers with applied coral dragons and tigers, red water bowls, white brush-washers, opaque white bamboo-shaped bottles painted with enamel, small round opaque white water pots, yellow bowls with handles, white *ruyi* scepters, red overlay water containers, three-legged opaque white and red overlay brush-washers, red overlay inkstone boxes, high-footed cups, three-legged horseshoe-shaped opaque white and red overlay brush-washers, and small bottles of jade green glass decorated with enamels.

The glass workshop continued to employ Kangxi styles and shapes into the Yongzheng reign. Colored glass imitated carnelian, jade and amber. Shapes occasionally imitated those of Ming dynasty lacquer, including chrysanthemum-petal bowls of the Jiajing period (1522-66) and cups with handles from the Xuande (1425-34) period. The Yongzheng emperor was anxious that the quality of his glass equal that of the Kangxi period. In his tenth year (1732), for example, the emperor ordered the duplication of some Kangxi-era water containers decorated in enamels with flowers on a gold ground. Later, the foreman Zhang Zicheng was forced to report that the workshop had failed.[36]

The collection of Yongzheng-era glass at the Palace Museum consists of only twelve pieces. Among the monochromes are light yellow, yellow, deep yellow, realgar, opaque white, translucent yellow, translucent light blue, and translucent purple. The shapes include an

1 Waterpot, transparent and faceted. Marked 'Kangxi yuzhi.'

2 Octagonal fluted vase, transparent blue. Marked 'Yongzheng nian zhi.'

3 Chrysanthemum-shaped *zhadou* (waste jar), yellow glass. Marked 'Yongzheng nian zhi.'

octagonal bottle (figure 2), a small bowl, a water jar, a *zhadou* waste jar (figure 3), and a round box. All bear the engraved mark 'Yongzheng nian zhi' (Made in the Yongzheng Reign), with characters arranged in two vertical rows. Although the quality of these pieces is good and their colors are bright, they are marred by the bubbles, striations, and pitting inevitable at the time. Nevertheless, as quality improved and productivity increased, glass became a common imperial gift for rulers and ambassadors of other countries. Glass had become not only an object of display for the court, but a state gift as well.

Qianlong Glass

Glassmaking reached its peak for a brief period in the Qianlong era after the steady progress made during the Kangxi and Yongzheng reigns. The most outstanding of Beijing products during this period were the commercially produced snuff bottles of the Xin, Le and Yuan factories. The Xin wares were the most refined, their monochrome colors bright and glittering. The factory made a type of snuff bottle known for a color like arrowroot, its translucent glass filled with tiny air bubbles. Most snuff bottles of this kind were overlaid with red, although multi-colored overlays also were produced. Some snuff bottles from the Le factory also had an arrowroot ground, with a mixed opaque and clear matrix like ice and snow. The Le factory surpassed the other two in the excellence of its imitation-gem colors. The Yuan snuff bottles had thin but heavy bodies, and grounds colored like seashell or gelatin, with multi-colored overlays. The reds and blues were brilliant, and the yellows had the richness of amber. The overlays were carved with scenes of 'The Land of the Immortals' and other motifs.[37]

Guangzhou continued to import glass from abroad and to manufacture it locally. According to the Englishman George Staunton,[38] during the Qianlong period at least some glassmakers in Guangzhou were content to melt and re-process fragments of imported glass which had been broken in shipment.

Products of the imperial glass workshop were particularly outstanding during the two decades from the fifth to the twenty-fourth year (1740-59) of the Qianlong reign. We know from the palace archives that at the beginning of the reign the workshop, still located in the summer palace, produced small items and occasionally striated snuff bottles. In the fifth year of Qianlong (1740), two Jesuit missionaries who would assist in glass production – Pierre d'Incarville and Gabriel-Léonard de Broussard – joined the court in Beijing.[39] The following year they produced aventurine glass and translucent blue glass.[40] During the seventeenth year of Qianlong (1752), a new furnace was built especially for making large pieces. From the twelfth month of Qianlong's seventeenth year (1752) to the third month of the following year – roughly a hundred days – the missionaries oversaw the production of three Western-style glass flowers, nine lanterns, eight bowls, and two watering pots, at the cost of some 3,349 taels of silver.[41] In the eighteenth year, they made three threaded-glass watering pots and one threaded brush holder.[42] In the twentieth year of his reign (1755), the emperor ordered five hundred glass snuff bottles and three thousand pieces of glass and utensils to be used as gifts at the summer palace at Chengde.[43] The following year, he ordered four pairs of multi-colored lanterns in imitation of the imported lanterns hanging in the hallways of Shui Fa Palace. The estimated cost for this project was 3,620 taels of silver.[44] The missionary court-painter Giuseppe Castiglione took charge of design, and de Broussard acted as technical director.

This situation did not last long. In the twenty-fifth year of his reign (1760), the emperor learned from his official Hai Wang that there were no longer any missionaries at court who were skilled in the techniques of glass blowing.[45] In the thirty-fifth year of the reign (1770), a certain Qi Libu carelessly broke the finial of a chandelier while setting up for a lantern festival. The emperor ordered a replacement from the imperial glass workshop, but the article originally had been made in the large furnace by missionaries, and the craftsmen were unable to duplicate it.[46] In the twelfth month of same year, Qianlong ordered two chandeliers. After seeing a scale model he asked his official Jin Hui, 'can it be done?' and the official reluctantly replied, 'barely.' The chandeliers, which were completed nine months later, incorporated five hundred and twelve fluted glass rods and cost 1,853 taels of silver. On orders from the emperor, the treasurer Wang De reduced the fee by one hundred and fifty-six taels on the grounds that the polishing was substandard.[47] This incident shows that Western missionaries were no longer associated with the imperial glass work-shop at this time, and that production had fallen below the high standards of the early years of the reign. The workshop now produced only snuff bottles and small items for use in New Year's and birthday festivities.

Qianlong glass differed from that of the Kangxi period. Having much in common with other contemporary arts, it was elaborate in shape and carved with detailed designs of dragons, phoenix, birds, fish, plants, landscapes, and human figures. The refined style of carving, similar to that used for jade, was described by Zhao Zhiqian as showing 'detail as fine as hair, with a ridge discernible to the touch.'[48]

The *guyuexuan* snuff bottle, another accomplishment of glassmaking in this era, remains something of a mystery. It was described as being the color of seashells, decorated in enamels with paintings and poems, and with the mark *guyuexuan* on the base. Those with the inscription 'Qianlong yu zhi' after the poem were the most highly regarded.[49] True *guyuexuan* snuff bottles are scarce as morning stars, and it is difficult to distinguish the authentic from the fake. Many articles published on this subject in recent years have done little to clarify the problem.

Glass from the Qianlong era survives in quantity. The Palace Museum, Beijing has a collection of several hundred examples, including incense burners, bottles, three-piece and five-piece altar sets, jars, basins, dishes, bowls, and snuff bottles. The collection can be surveyed according to four categories:

Monochromes
Monochrome glass includes opaque white, seashell white, pale yellow, light yellow, real-gar, transparent tea color, transparent tea yellow, moon-white, royal blue, sky blue, trans-parent light blue, transparent dark blue, transparent dark red, transparent rose red, transparent ruby red, peach red, pea green, light green, red-bean purple, light purple, transparent dark purple, clear crystal, and tea crystal.

Polychromes
- Aventurine: gold flecks in a dark tea or red-brown glass
- Speckled colors: pieces of colored glass pressed into a ground, such as black sprinkled with gold flecks; black spotted with gold flecks; turquoise spotted with gold flecks; a

black ground pressed with aventurine glass; or yellow, red, and multiple colors forming a ground with speckled colors, such as mixed brownish-red with yellow-green as a ground, pressed with yellow streaked with red; or a mixture of blue, white, green, and yellow as ground, spotted with aventurine

- Sandwiched gold: gold flecks embedded in a black or dark blue ground, covered with transparent glass (figure 4)[50]
- Sandwiched color: an opaque white ground speckled with gold, green, and blue spots, covered with light green transparent glass
- Threaded or Striated: alternately light and dark monochromatic mixtures, such as water lily green, rosy purple, and dark opaque green; and polychrome mixtures (figure 5), including opaque white mixed with green, bright red with yellow, royal blue with white, aventurine, pea yellow with dark red and light green

Tao liao ('cased' or overlay glass):
- A clear or opaque white ground cased with color: opaque white cased with blue (figure 6), red (figure 7),[51] dark red or light green;[52] clear glass cased with dark blue
- Colored glass cased with colors: pale yellow ground cased with red (figure 8), royal blue cased with opaque green, a grey ground cased with dark yellow, peach red cased with arrowroot, green cased with dark blue
- Opaque white ground cased with multiple layers: opaque ground cased with moon-white, purple, and burgundy

4 Small jar, gold-flecked blue. Qing period.
5 Vase, striped glass. Marked 'Qianlong nian zhi.'
6 Bowl, opaque white with blue overlay carved in lotus decoration. Marked 'Qianlong nian zhi.'

7 Vase, opaque white with red overlay carved in pattern of two dragons. Qianlong mark.
8 Covered stemcup, pale yellow ground with red overlay carved in floral motifs and longevity symbols. Qianlong period.

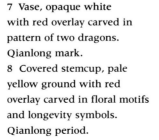

- Colored ground cased with multiple layers: ivory yellow ground cased with dark blue and dark red
- Speckled ground cased with multiple layers: opaque white with red spots cased with dark red, transparent green, and transparent blue

Decoration
- Carving: done by jade craftsmen; incising or relief carving[53]
- Cold-painted colors: scenes painted on transparent or gold-flecked grounds[54]
- Painted gold: gold painted on transparent glass
- Gold lines: engraved lines filled with gold
- Painted enamel: usually enamel painted on an opaque white ground and fired[55]

From this overview of the Palace Museum's collection, it is evident that Qianlong glass has much in common with the less refined Yongzheng glass, although the pieces also have their share of bubbles, striations, and pitting.

Glass from Jiaqing to Xuantong

A century's decline in imperial glassmaking began with the start of the Jiaqing reign (1796-1820), as the workshop came to produce little more than offerings for the New Year's festivities and other such occasions. In keeping with a practice established by the start of the Yongzheng reign, the imperial glass factory, like other units of the Zaobanchu, presented gifts to the emperor during the Dragon Boat (Duanwu), Mid-Autumn, New Year's, and imperial birthday festivals. In the Yongzheng and early Qianlong reigns, no set number of gifts was required for these festivals. Early in the Jiaqing reign, glass offered each year for the Duanwu and New Year's festivals totaled three hundred and one pieces: one hundred and eighty-one dishes, bowls, wine cups, and saucers, and one hundred and twenty snuff bottles. In the twenty-fifth year of Jiaqing (1820), the offering was reduced to one hundred dishes, bowls, wine cups, and saucers, and sixty snuff bottles. The number returned to three hundred and one during the Daoguang reign, but the quality did not compare with that of the Qianlong and Jiaqing periods.

The craftsmen continued to be recruited from Boshan. For example, the brothers He Zhen and He Lan, both glassblowers from Boshan, were at the imperial workshop from the seventeenth to the twenty-second year of the Jiaqing reign (1812-17), while the brothers He Lan and He Hai appear in documents after the twenty-second year of the reign.[56] For the remainder of the century, with few exceptions, two glassblowers would work for three to five months to finish the quota of three hundred and one pieces and then return to Boshan. Sometimes even this limited quota had to be reduced by half, or production ceased altogether for a period of a year or more.

Glassmaking under Jiaqing inherited the styles of the Qianlong period, even maintaining the general standard of late Qianlong glass, but in the Daoguang era (1821-50), glassmaking sank to a low level. Pieces were oddly shaped, the contours ill-defined; those with applied decoration were particularly poor. Even the reign marks were done carelessly. In the eighth year (1858) of the Xianfeng reign, the emperor ordered that the workshop 'make only simple, undecorated wares; the mark must be clearly rendered.'[57] Glass during the reigns of Tongzhi (1862-74) and Guangxu (1875-1908) showed some improvement over Daoguang glass, but carved glass did not again enter production.

Boshan and commercial factories in Beijing proved more successful than the imperial glass workshop. The Scottish missionary Alexander Williamson wrote in 1870 that a local rock mixed with saltpeter was used in making Boshan glass.[58] The products included window glass, bottles, molded cups, lanterns, beads, and other ornaments. The glass also was made into 'rods about thirty inches long, which they tie up in bundles and export to all parts of the country.' Prices were very reasonable. Williamson praised the glass as 'extremely pure; they colour it most beautifully, and have attained considerable dexterity in manipulation; many of the articles were finely finished.'

In the late nineteenth century, whole families including women and children were still participating in the trade. Crowded factories and furnaces were located on the outskirts of town. Such Boshan glass products as jade imitations and roof tiles sold well in Beijing. But the Qing government, in an effort to control profits from glass production, promulgated laws to prevent merchants from stocking merchandise, threatening them with fines and confiscation of their goods. This kind of restriction damaged production and even brought on riots in Boshan.[59] In the twenty-eighth year of the Guangxu reign (1902), thousands of workers destroyed the building of a company that had been formed by the official Zhao Erhua to monopolize glass production. The struggle was suppressed. In the thirtieth year of Guangxu (1904), as part of a new governmental policy, Hu Tinggan, a high official in Shandong, founded a glass company at Liukang, northeast of Boshan. The factory, which produced glass of satisfactory quality, was shut down towards the end of the Xuantong reign (1908-11). Local Chinese craftsmen, having learned new techniques from seven German glassmen at the factory, opened their own facility on Xiye Street to produce the first locally-made sheet glass in Boshan.

The glassmaking industry in Beijing benefited greatly from the period of relative stability, known as the Tongzhi Restoration, which followed the suppression of the Taiping rebellion in 1864. Glass factories generally offered their finest pieces to the emperor, and the Palace Museum's collection of Peking glass from this period consists of mostly small, delicate items of high quality. The products include imitation sapphire and jade rings of striking color and transparency, but the most outstanding pieces are snuff bottles. Multi-layered glass reached as many as seven colors, as in a snuff bottle with an opaque white ground covered with moon-white, mottled orange and brown, beeswax, dark blue, pink, and rose red. Interior-painted bottles were popular throughout China. During the Guangxu reign, the work of the famous Zhou Leyuan and Ye Zhongsan reached the inner quarters of the imperial palace and their techniques became known in Boshan. Press-mold techniques also developed in this period to take the place of the work of jade craftsmen. Colored glass was laid over a transparent or opaque white body and then pressed with a patterned mold. This saved time and money, but the quality of the relief decoration was not comparable to that of carved wares. Imitations of *guyuexuan* snuff bottles were made in considerable quantity in this period, although they were rarely of high quality.[60]

Conclusion

Based on documentation and the study of the Palace Museum collection, this essay has surveyed the production, distribution, and development of Qing dynasty glass. However, in the lengthy history of Qing glass, many questions remain unanswered. Three areas require further examination.

The relationship between the imperial glass workshop and local factories

The development of the imperial workshop seems to have depended on the strength of the local factories, particularly for the contribution of technical skill and raw materials. But in each period, due to the demands and resources of the emperor, the level of production of the imperial workshop far exceeded that of local glass factories.

The conclusion that Qing dynasty glassmaking reached its peak during the Qianlong reign is based on the production records of the imperial workshop. The development of glassmaking at Guangzhou, Boshan and, outside the court, at Beijing is poorly documented. Nevertheless, it has been demonstrated that during the period when the imperial glass workshop reached its peak, the materials and technical skills came from Boshan.

The relationship between foreign and indigenous glassmaking techniques

In surveying the history of Qing dynasty glassmaking, we can confirm that traditional techniques were predominant. Although foreign techniques were introduced and adapted in this period, they were not the norm, nor were they more than temporary. An interplay between foreign and Chinese glassmaking techniques had existed also in ancient times.

This essay has suggested that techniques from abroad hastened the development of Qing glass. Based on reliable sources, we have seen how glass was imported via Guangzhou; how the missionary de Broussard produced a range of Western-style glass, and how the Boshan craftsmen learned the technique of manufacturing sheet glass from German glassmen. Foreign techniques were helpful at different periods in stimulating and improving traditional Chinese glassmaking, but they neither completely replaced traditional techniques nor affected the traditional styles of Chinese glass.[61]

The imperial impact on glass production

This is a question of the relationship between court and popular art, a relationship which exists in all crafts under the management of the Palace Workshop. A great deal of documentation supports the idea that the emperor's interests influenced the production of all court products; glassmaking, of course, was no exception. The products of local factories depended on another audience, the wider public, and were not directly affected by imperial demands. Indirectly, the art of the court did influence other factories, as illustrated by the numerous imitations of imperial-style glass of the golden age from Kangxi to Qianlong. The craftsmen who had made glass at the imperial workshop no doubt introduced the court styles and techniques to Boshan upon their return. The situation was reversed at the end of the Qing dynasty, when products of local factories poured into the palace for the emperor's enjoyment.

Notes

1 See Yang Boda, 'Xizhou boli di yanjiu,' *Gugong bowuyuan yuankan* (1980, no. 2): 14-24.

2 Shangguan Bi, 'Boli gongyi de lishi tantao,' *Meishu yanjiu* (1960, no. 10); also Yang Boda, 'Guanyu woguo gu bolishi yanjiu zhong de jige wenti,' *Wenwu* (1979, no. 5): 76-78.

3 Sun Tingquan, *Yanshan zaji*, in *Siku quanshu*, series 5, vol. 102, *juan* 4: 7-12.

4 Xiang Da, 'Ming Qing zhiji Zhongguo meishu suoshou Xiyang yingxiang,' *Tangdai Changan yu Xiyu wenming* (Beijing, 1957): 495-531.

5 E'ertai, Zhang Tingyu et al., ed., *Daqing Shizong xianhuangdi shilu* (preface dated 1741), *juan* 99: 2-3, entry under the eighth year of Yongzheng, tenth month, *gengzi*.

6 Scattered references can be found in Wei Zheng et al., *Suishu, juan* 68, entry He Chou; and Zhou Mi, *Wulin jiushi, juan* 2, in *Dongjing menghua lu* (Shanghai, 1956).

7 Song Yingxing, *Tiangong kaiwu* (Shanghai, 1954), final chapter.

8 Sun Tingqian, *Yanshan zaji*, 7.

9 *Yanshan Sunshi zupu* (1749), in Zibo Municipal Library.

10 On 27 October 1982, Bi Siliang, of the Zibo Municipal Museum, Shandong, discovered the remains of a glasshouse at the site of the First Market Place in Bocheng (formerly Boshan xian). Bi Siliang gathered a small number of saltpeter jars and some glass shards. Yang Jingrong, Gao Aizhen, Zhang Fengrong and I were able to examine these on the afternoon of 3 December. We regarded this as the first discovery of the remains of a glasshouse in China. During the same visit, we also examined seventeen pieces of Yuan ceramics discovered in the outer eastern wall of the site, including Jun, Longquan and Shufu wares inscribed in Basiba language. The following day, we arrived at Boshan, accompanied by Luo Xunzhang of the [Shandong] Provincial Archaeological Institute; Wang Naiming of the Cultural Relics Department, [Zibo] Municipal Cultural Bureau; Bi Siliang, Zhang Guangming and Liu Zhongjin of the Zibo Municipal Museum; and Cai Yinghai of the Municipal Political Cooperative. We went to the site immediately and again on the morn-

ings of 5 and 6 December, when we gathered samples of glass, burned charcoal, broken pieces of saltpeter jars, glass threads, hairpins, beads and the like. Bi Siliang and Zhang Guangming began to catalog this material. According to their report, there were ten foundry sites or ashpits. Gao Aizhen excavated a Ming copper coin marked with the legend 'Hongwu tongbao.' From a stratigraphical standpoint, and in light of the evidence from coinage and Yuan ceramics, this glasshouse can be dated around the late Yuan to early Ming. Analysis of the glass shards found that they contain a high level of calcium and a low level of lead.

11 The tomb of Zhu Tan (died twenty-second year of Hongwu, 1389) yielded black and white gaming pieces for *weiqi*. See Shandong Provincial Museum, 'Fajue Ming Zhu Tan mu jishi,' *Wenwu* (1972, no. 5): 25-36.

12 Du En and Feng Weina, *Qingzhou fuzhi* (1565; Shanghai, 1965 reprint).

13 Sun Tingquan, *Yanshan zaji*, 8-10.

14 See Stephen W. Bushell, *Chinese Art* (London, 1909), 2: 62; also Wang Yingui and Zhang Xinzeng, *Xuxiu Boshan xianzhi* (1937). Xiye Street is mentioned in Fu Shen and Tian Shilin, *Boshan xianzhi* (1753).

15 Gao Lian, *Zunsheng bajian*, in *Meishu congshu*, third *ji, ji* 10: 161.

16 Ge Hong, *Baopuzi neiwaibian, juan* 2, *neibian*, 'On Immortals,' 7.

17 For example, *Nanzhou yiwu zhi* and *Taiping yulan*, as cited in Ruan Yuan, Chen Changqi and others, *Guangdong tongzhi* (1864), *juan* 94: 3-4.

18 *Documents of Production of Yangxin Hall Palace Workshops, Imperial Household Department of the Qing Dynasty* (hereafter cited as *Documents*): Yongzheng 6th year, document no. 3313. This is preserved in the Zhongguo Diyi Lishi Dangan Guan (First Historical Archive of China).

19 *Documents*, Qianlong 21st year, no. 3475.

20 Liang Tongshu, *Gu tongciqi kao*, in *Meishu congshu*, first *ji, ji* 5: 161.

21 Kun Gang et al., *Qinding Daqing huidian shili* (1899 edition), *juan* 1173.

22 Bushell, *Chinese Art*, 2: 62.

23 Alexander Williamson, *Journeys in North China, Manchuria and Eastern Mongolia*, (London, 1870), 1: 131-32.

24 Liang Tongshu, *Gu tongciqi kao*, 161.

25 Wang Chong, *Lunheng*, in *Congshu jicheng chubian*, 'Shuaixing.'

26 Yan Shigu, commentary on the *Qian Hanshu, juan* 96: 11, 'Xiyu zhuan,' on *liuli* production in the state of Jibin.

27 Zhao Rugua, *Zhufan zhi, juan* 2: 11.

28 *Qingzhou fuzhi.*

29 *Documents*, Qianlong 17th year, no. 3438.

30 Sun Tingquan, *Yanshan zaji*, 7-8.

31 *Suzhou fuzhi* (1824), on imperial visits, *juan shou* 1: 33.

32 Zhao Zhiqian, *Yonglu xianjie*, in *Meishu congshu*, first *ji, ji* 3: 215.

33 Zhao Zhiqian, *Yonglu xianjie*, 215; Wang Shizhen's comment from his *Xiangzu biji* (1702) is quoted by Zhao, 214.

34 For additional illustrations of glass in the Palace Museum, as well as reference photographs of their reign marks, the reader is referred to the original Chinese text.

35 *Documents*, Yongzheng 3rd year, no. 3294.

36 *Documents*, Yongzheng 10th year, no. 3348.

37 Zhao Zhiqian, *Yonglu xianjie*, 215.

38 George Staunton, *An Authentic Account of an Embassy from the King of Great Britain to the Emperor of China* (London, 1797), 2: 288.

39 *Documents*, Qianlong seventh year, no. 3399. [Editor's Note: The missionaries' Chinese names given by Yang are Ji Wen and Wang Zhizhong. The first is identifiable as the Jesuit lay-brother Gabriel-Léonard de Broussard, in China from 1740 until his death in 1758. Born in Chartres in 1703 and trained as a glassman, he was described by a fellow missionary in 1754 as producing 'glass in the best taste and most difficult in execution, which shines today in the Throne Room beside the finest works from France and England' (see Louis Pfister, *Notices biographiques et bibliographiques sur les Jesuites de l'ancienne mission de Chine, 1552-1773* [Shanghai, 1932], 801). The name Wang Zhizhong apparently is a mistranscription for Tang Zhizhong, the Jesuit priest Pierre d'Incarville, who accompanied de Broussard to China and pursued a variety of scientific interests at court until his death in 1757 (see Pfister, *Notices biographiques*, 795-99).]

40 *Documents*, Qianlong 6th year, nos. 3395, 3392.

41 *Documents*, Qianlong 21st year, no. 3475.

42 *Documents*, Qianlong 18th year, no. 3442.

43 *Documents*, Qianlong 20th year, no. 3465.

44 *Documents*, Qianlong 21st year, no. 3493.

45 *Documents*, Qianlong 25th year, no. 3509.

46 *Documents*, Qianlong 35th year, no. 3565.

47 Ibid.

48 Zhao Zhiqian, *Yonglu xianjie*, 215.

49 Zhao Zhiqian, *Yonglu xianjie*, 215-16.

50 See pp. 77 and 89 of this catalog.

51 See also Chinese text, pl. 2, no.2.

52 Illustrated in Chinese text, pl. 2, no. 1.

53 Illustrated in Chinese text, pl. 2, no. 5.

54 Illustrated in Chinese text, pl. 3, no. 1.

55 Illustrated in Chinese text, pl. 3, nos. 2, 3.

56 *Shandong xunfu ziwen*, preserved in the First Historical Archive of China. Jiaqing twenty-second year, second month, eleventh day.

57 *Documents*, Xianfeng 8th year, no. 3078.

58 Williamson, *Journeys*, 1: 131-32.

59 *North China Herald* (27 January 1903), quoted in Bushell, *Chinese Art*, 2: 62.

60 Illustrated in Chinese text, pl. 3, nos. 4, 5.

61 On a visit to the Zibo Meishu Boli Chang (Zibo Art Glassworks) in Boshan district in 1982, the author learned from deputy factory director Zhang Xuan that the factory mainly employs raw materials brought in from outside, using soda ash as a flux, rather than, as during the Qing dynasty, relying on local materials. According to senior craftsmen at the factory, a soda ash flux was already in use before 1949. This coincides with the ingredients listed by Zhi Lian, 'Boshan liaohuo ji taoqi,' *Guomin zazhi* (1941, no. 10). Differences in the raw materials, chemical ingredients and fuels used in Boshan now, as opposed to during the Qing dynasty, account for differences in color and physical characteristics.

Qing Enameled Glass

Chang Lin-sheng, Curator
Department of Antiquities
National Palace Museum
Taipei

In China, the terms *boli*, *liuli*, and *liaoqi* were applied, respectively, to transparent, translucent, and opaque glass, although the usage was not always consistent. The term *liangliang'er*, which was derived phonetically from *liuli*, referred traditionally to glass products first made in Boshan, Shandong Province and in later times produced also in Beijing. Objects that bore this name were mostly decorative items for use by women, such as hairpins, bracelets, and earrings. According to Qi Rushan (1876-1962),[1] during the Qing dynasty there were many in rural areas who peddled *liangliang'er* from wooden trays which displayed an array of bright and colorful items. In the last years of the dynasty, Peking glass production replaced these women's ornaments with vases, jars, dishes, and bowls, which were in heavy demand.

A passage in *The Dream of the Red Chamber* (mid-eighteenth century) provides the information that 'In Fulangsiya in the West there were accounts of a gold-star gem made of glass. In the original language, this gold gem was called *wendu lina*.' In his investigation of the Western artifacts recorded in *The Dream of the Red Chamber*, Fang Hao identified 'Fulangsiya' as an alternate rendering of Folangji (France). In French, a pane of glass for a window or cabinet is a 'vitrine,' phonetically similar to *wendu lina*.[2] At any rate, it appears that during the Qing dynasty, imported glass was also known by the name of *wendu lina*.[3] According to documents of the Zaobanchu, or Palace Workshop, in the sixth year of Qianlong (1741), Western missionaries in the court assisted in the production of *wendu lina*. Thus, it would seem that the designation may also be applied to Chinese imitations of Western glass.

During the Qing dynasty, glass was known by the varied names of *boli*, *liuli*, *liaoqi* *liangliang'er*, *wendu lina* and *shao liao*, clouded or frosted glass. To further complicate matters, in old documents the term *liuli* also was applied to natural gems and to ceramic glazes.

Glass Production in the Palace Workshop

The development of glassmaking at court reflects the Kangxi emperor's personal interest in Western science and craft. During his reign, Western emissaries bearing tribute to China or missionaries intending to spread religious messages often brought with them precious and exotic objects as gifts. Joining the clocks, watches, and other scientific instruments was glass, the exquisite craftsmanship of which rendered it one of the most highly regarded types of tribute. According to the *Chibei outan* (Chibei miscellany) of the poet and official Wang Shizhen (1634-1711),[4] in the sixth year of Kangxi (1667), tribute presented by a Dutch mission included glass boxes in addition to knives, swords, horses, and white oxen. In the twenty-fifth year of Kangxi (1686), Dutch tribute included two large mirrors, five hundred and eighty-one *liuli* cups of various shapes, one large *liuli* lamp, one [chandelier?], and one large striking-clock, in addition to such items as clove, camphor, nutmeg, cassia oil, and grape wine. The historian He Qiutao (1824-62) records in his *Shuofang beicheng* (Historical sourcebook of the northern regions) that in the fifteenth year of Kangxi (1676), Russia presented the tribute of mirrors.[5] According to *Xichao ding'an* (Episodes of a prosperous age), in the second month, twenty-eighth year of Kangxi (1689), the emperor, having reached Hangzhou during his Southern Tour, received from the Jesuit Prosper Intorcetta the gift of a polychrome glass sphere; and having arrived in Suzhou, received from another missionary a small telescope, a facial mirror, and two glass vases.[6]

Originally published as
'Qingchao de boli liaoqi'
(Glass of the Qing Dynasty)
Gugong wenwu yuekan, vol. 1,
no. 9 (December 1985): 4-13.
Translation by Ju-hsi
Chou. Edited and adapted by
by Donald Rabiner.

Pieces illustrated in this essay
are in the collection of
the National Palace Museum.

These gifts from the West appealed immensely to the Kangxi emperor by virtue of their color and lustre, and may have stimulated him to establish the imperial glass workshop within the palace compound.

Within the Forbidden City, the Palace Workshop, which belonged to the Imperial Household Department and was headquartered in Yangxin Hall, was charged with manufacturing court utensils and paraphernalia. Its precursors include the Shangfang Jian (Directorate for Imperial Manufactories) of the Han dynasty, the Shaofu Jian (Directorate for Imperial Manufactories) of the Tang dynasty and the Yuyong Jian (Directorate for Imperial Accouterments) of the Ming dynasty. In the thirty-second year of his reign (1693), Kangxi expanded the Palace Workshop, establishing fourteen craft studios devoted to such items as cloisonné, clocks, guns, and maps, and including the Ruyiguan (Institute of Indulgences), to which were attached painters and craftsmen skilled in jade, bamboo, and ivory carving, embroidery, and carpentry. Craftsmen in each studio were appointed by officers of the Imperial Household Department. Southern craftsmen were recommended by the Imperial Silk Manufactory in Suzhou and by the superintendent's office of the Guangdong Customs House.[7]

According to *Daqing huidian shili* (Collected sub-statutes of the Qing), the glass workshop was established as a division of the Palace Workshop by imperial edict in the thirty-fifth year of Kangxi (1696). Its personnel included a part-time secretary in addition to the glassmakers and blowers. Of the blowers, two were regularly appointed by the Office of Palace Construction through the recommendation of the governor of Shandong. In the forty-seventh year of Kangxi (1708), an edict reassigned craftsmen from Yangxin Hall to the Zaobanchu's Imperial Food Service in Cining Hall. The forty-ninth year of Kangxi (1710) saw within the glass workshop the appointment of two work superintendents and one additional *bitieshi*, or bannerman-clerk. The fifty-sixth year of Kangxi (1717) witnessed the further addition of two work superintendents and another *bitieshi*. In the eleventh year of Yongzheng (1733), a post for a deputy storehouse keeper was added to the office of the work superintendents. The following year, a deputy secretary joined the personnel. In the fifth year of Qianlong (1740), a request was approved to appoint a deputy foreman from among the *baitang'a*, or apprentices, in the glass workshop. The following year, approval was given to add one more deputy foreman from the ranks of apprentices, as well as three more deputy storekeepers and six more deputy foremen.[8]

In view of the above, as documented in memorials and edicts through the three reigns of Kangxi (1662-1722), Yongzheng (1723-35) and Qianlong (1736-95), we can conclude that the imperial glass workshop was characterized by steady progress and expansion.

Glassmaking during the Kangxi Reign

In the third month, forty-second year of Kangxi (1703), when the emperor undertook his fourth Southern Tour, he encountered Gao Shiqi (1645-1703), a former official who had retired to his native place at Huai'an. Mindful of his earlier fondness for the man, the emperor asked him to accompany the entourage back to the capital and bestowed upon him gifts and honors. One day, he summoned Gao Shiqi to Yangxin Hall, and commanded him to look around. Within the interior of the Hall, where the display of paintings and books remained unchanged, the emperor directed him to come near to the couch to examine 'the newly-made glass, which is refined and lustrous.' Seeking to please, Gao Shiqi observed: 'Even though these are [a form of] pottery, their success or failure reflects on the government. Now China can produce [glass] far surpassing that of the West.' Delighted by his response, the emperor bestowed upon the former official some twenty pieces of glass. Unfortunately, the nature and appearance of these newly-made pieces was not recorded.[9]

In the forty-fourth year of Kangxi (1705), the emperor undertook his fifth Southern Tour. In Suzhou he summoned Governor Song Luo (1634-1713), whose fame in poetry approached that of Wang Shizhen. The list of imperial gifts given to Song Luo on this occasion includes seventeen items of glass and, like the gifts to Gao Shiqi, attests to the great strides the workshop appears to have made within a decade of its establishment in the Forbidden City in 1696.[10]

1 Vase with painted enamel decoration. Kangxi period.

According to another text by Wang Shizhen, the *Xiangzu biji* (Orchid fragrance notes), the colors in Kangxi glass include red, purple, green, yellow, black, and white.[11] It could be 'clear as crystal, red as flame.' Among the imperial gifts to Song Luo, the *Suzhou fuzhi* (Gazetteer of Suzhou Prefecture) recorded blue glass and blue glass flecked with gold; the latter may have been an attempt to imitate lapis lazuli.

An important example of Kangxi glass is a small vase of gall bladder shape measuring 12.5 cm in height and weighing 146.1 gm (figure 1). Its shape, with bloated belly and constricted neck, is similar to that found in Kangxi porcelain. Painted enamel decoration covers the entire surface; against a background of indigo blue are intertwining peonies, the petals of which are painted with burnt siena, pink, and apple green, while the branches and leaves are colored with light yellow and pale brown. The decoration is similar to that on Kangxi painted enamels on both porcelain and copper: stately and exquisite, without being unduly decorative. A comparison with Qianlong-period examples reveals that the body of this Kangxi piece is much lighter in weight. The shape of the base and the curvature of the indentation differ from those of the Yongzheng and Qianlong periods, and the base is neither incised nor painted with enamel. The milk-white surface is not smooth and clear, but bears a network of tiny pits. In that respect, it is unlike Qianlong pieces where the glass body has the consistent texture of lard. Perhaps to conceal the blemishes, the surface is fully covered in painted decor.

The scholar-artist Zhao Zhiqian (1829-84), in his *Yonglu xianjie*,[12] mentioned as an innovation in Kangxi glass the production of *tao liao*, cased or overlay glass:

> At the time the empire was peaceful and rich with ten thousand things. Arts and crafts sought to achieve elegance. Therefore many styles, from plain to elaborate, were present. There was, in addition, a new technique in glass-making called *tao*, or casing, so-called because the colors were cased onto a plain background.

Some Kangxi glassmakers applied a single layer of color to a plain glass body. Others cased in multiple layers of different hues on a monochrome body. The colors included red, blue, green, black, and white. In terms of skill in carving and engraving, the results often are unparalleled in quality.

In the fifty-ninth year of Kangxi (1720), Giovanni Ambrogio Mezzabarba, an emissary from Clement XI, arrived in Beijing bearing gifts. In return, the emperor sent the pope the following: a cloisonné box, ten cloisonné vases, one hundred and twenty-eight ceramic vases of various sizes, one hundred and thirty-six 'glass vases of Beijing,' and sixteen scroll paintings. Unfortunately, on the journey back, this selection of gifts perished with the emissary in a fire in Rio de Janeiro, and these one hundred and thirty-six vases, which may well have been a summation of the achievement of late Kangxi glassmaking, were irretrievably lost.[13]

Glassmaking during the Yongzheng Era

During the Yongzheng period, the imperial glass workshop, together with the other units under the jurisdiction of the Zaobanchu, was moved to the Yuanming Yuan summer palace. According to the *Zaobanchu huoji dang* (Palace workshop production records), the glass workshop's output included opaque white bamboo-shaped bottles painted with enamels, grape-colored cups, semi-opaque red cups, white brush-washers, yellow bowls with handles, white *ruyi* scepters, opaque-yellow beads, large cased red bowls, and cased red inkstone boxes. A painted snuff bottle in the shape of a bamboo stalk, exquisitely fashioned with an opaque white body (figure 2), bears an ingenious 'Yongzheng nian zhi' mark on the base, the four characters emerging from an auspicious pattern of purple fungi.

Glassmaking during the Qianlong Reign

As Yongzheng's successor, the Qianlong emperor saw to it that glass remained in production in the Yuanming Yuan. As early as his princely days, the future emperor had versified upon seeing a glass plate:

> Its purity matches mica's,
> In radiance it rivals crystal.[14]

To improve the quality of the glass, Qianlong relied upon Western missionaries skilled in glassmaking and ordered his craftsmen to imitate Western decorative patterns and shapes. The missionaries assisted in the design and construction of large furnaces, and seem to have had a role in changing the chemical composition of the glass itself.

Qianlong-period enameled glass is known for its refinement. In terms of weight, the pieces are heavier than those of the Kangxi and Yongzheng eras. The body is lustrous and clear, without blemishes. On enameled pieces, the *kaishu* (regular script) inscription of 'Qianlong nian zhi' usually is written in enamels rather than incised. A faceted vase with *fushou* (felicity and longevity) decoration measures 13.2 cm in height and weighs 270.8 gm; the body is of a translucent pigeon-egg white (figure 3). Against a background of light yellow enamel, on each of the rhomboidal surfaces, five bats (*fu*) surround the character of *shou* to complete the symbolism. The intervening triangular surfaces are decorated with flowering plants, while banana leaves surround the neck. The enameled reign mark runs laterally along the outer surface of the foot.

A vase depicting the theme of 'tutoring the child' has a height of 10.4 cm and weighs 202 gm (figure 4). The base has a rare incised inscription. In a garden, mother and child sit against a rock. Head tilted and with a finger touching her chin, the mother attempts to

2 Bamboo-shaped snuff bottle with painted enamel decoration. Enameled mark 'Yongzheng nian zhi.'
3 Faceted vase with painted enamel decoration. Enameled mark 'Qianlong nian zhi.'
4 Vase with painted enamel decoration. Incised mark 'Qianlong nian zhi.'

teach the child to read – a conventional subject in the Ming and Qing periods. The rendering of the figures and background is detailed and elegant. The poetic lines read:

> From the tips of twigs, the moon shines over the infinite.
> Autumn is not far when blooms reach their peak.

Vignettes of landscape, flora, and fauna had already begun to appear during the Yongzhong era in painted enamel and in *fencai* (famille rose) porcelain, often coupled with poetic lines. This fashion constituted an extension of *wenren* (scholarly) sentiment into the imperial wares, as a means to mitigate what otherwise might be considered merely superficial beauty.

A *zhadou*, or waste jar, 7.5 cm high and weighing 227.3 gm, is decorated with Western figures (figure 5). The ivory-white body was shaped by means of a mold, as attested to by the seam that resulted from a slight mismatching of the mold pieces. In the belly portion, a framed cartouche surrounded by white floral and brocade-like patterns opens to a scene of Western figures in repose. This typifies an aspect of Qianlong style which is frequently seen in the painted enamels of this period.

A gourd-shaped vase, decorated with a scene of children at play, measures 11.1 cm in height and weighs 212.1 gm (figure 6). The body is of an off-white, pigeon-egg shade. The enameled decoration is divided into two zones. Above, a sepia-colored landscape is accompanied by the poetic line, 'A village of green hovers near a clear stream.' Below, the traditional scene of 'children at play' contains three figures frolicking in the garden, one holding a bamboo branch, another with a peach branch and the third with a *wan* symbol and a twin-fish toy. A second gourd-shaped vase, bearing the symbolic motifs of 'five fortunes through ten thousand generations,' measures 7.8 cm in height and weighs 80.4 gm (figure 7). The gourd vines (*man*) of the decoration creep and casually wind their way around the entire surface. Since one gourd plant may produce hundreds of gourds, the vine carries the symbolic meaning of having many children and grandchildren; in addition, *man* sounds similar to *wan* (ten thousand). An image of gourds trailing the creeping vines thus suggests *zisun wandai* (ten thousand generations of descendants). Augmenting this symbolism is the depiction of five bats, the pictorial equivalent of fortune (*fu*). The combined signification is *wufu wandai* (five fortunes through ten thousand generations).

5 *Zhadou* with painted enamel decoration. Enameled mark 'Qianlong nian zhi.'
6 Gourd-shaped vase with painted enamel decoration. Enameled mark 'Qianlong nian zhi.'
7 Gourd-shaped vase with painted enamel decoration. Qianlong period.

The gourd shape of these glass vases reflects a long tradition in China. From the Northern Wei period, a stone container buried under the foundation of the pagoda in Dingxian, Hebei, yielded three small gourd-shaped glass vases.[15] Light blue in color and transparent, the vases had spherical bellies and long necks. A celadon gourd-shaped *zun* was found in the Tang tomb of Liu Jiaqu, Shanxian, Henan. From the Sung period, the foundation of the Huiguang pagoda yielded a silver vase of gourd shape; beneath the foundation of the pagoda in Haiqingsi, Lianyun Gang, was found a celadon gourd vase; and from the foundations of two pagodas in Dingxian came several hundred glass gourd vases. During the Ming and Qing periods, the glass factories in Boshan also produced gourd vases in large quantities.

Zhao Zhiqian described the famous *guyuexuan* as a ware whose white glass body was decorated in enamel colors and included poetic lines, as well as the inscription *guyuexuan* at the foot. He added that 'those with the legend of "Qianlong nian zhi" were especially beautiful.'[16] The so-called *guyuexuan*, well-known among connoisseurs, is it not this very type of delightful and exquisitely painted glass?

Notes

1 Qi Rushan, 'Zhongguo guyoude huaxue gongyi,' in *Qi Rushan quanji* (Taipei, 1979), 9: 5232.

2 Fang Hao, 'Cong *Honglou meng* suo ji Xiyang wupin kao gushi de beijing,' in *Fang Hao liushi ziding gao* (Taipei, 1969), *juan* 1: 425-26.

3 Editor's Note: Fang Hao's article was reprinted in *Honglou meng yanjiu zhuankan* (1970, no. 7): 13-14. In the same issue of the journal, Li Zhihua argued persuasively for deriving *wendu lina* from the French 'aventurine,' a type of glass which contains sparkling, gold-like particles of copper or chromic oxide. The term can also refer to a translucent quartz with specks of mica. See 'Wendu lina yici yuanwen de shangque,' *Honglou meng yanjiu zhuankan* (1970, no. 7): 95-96.

4 Wang Shizhen, *Chibei outan*, in *Biji xiaoshuo daguan* (Taipei, 1978-83), second *bian*, 8: 4553-54.

5 He Qiutao, *Shuofang beicheng*, in *Biji xiaoshuo daguan*, thirteenth *bian*, 8: 5197.

6 *Xichao Ding'an*, in *Tianzhujiao dongchuan wenxian xu bian* (Taipei, 1966 reprint), *juan* 3: 1757, 1762.

7 *Qinding Daqing huidian shili* (Taipei, 1963 reprint), *juan* 1214: 17.

8 *Qinding Daqing huidian shili*, *juan* 1173: 4-7.

9 Gao Shiqi, *Pengshan miji*, in *Manzhou yeshi* (Taipei, 1972 reprint), *juan* 7: 2453.

10 Feng Guifen et al., *Suzhou fuzhi* (Taipei, 1970 reprint), 1: 50.

11 Wang Shizhen, *Xiangzu biji*, in *Biji xiaoshuo daguan*, twenty-eighth *bian*, 5: 3054-55.

12 Zhao Zhiqian, *Yonglu xianjie*, in *Meishu congshu*, first *ji*, *ji* 3: 215.

13 George Loehr, 'Missionary Artists at the Manchu Court,' *Transactions of the Oriental Ceramic Society* 34 (1962-63): 57, nn. 33, 34.

14 *Leshantang quanji*, in *Qing Gaozong yuzhi shiwen quanji* (Taipei, 1976), vol. 1, *juan* 24: 13.

15 See Chang Lin-sheng, 'Shishen woguo liuli gongyi fazhan shi shang de wenti,' *Gugong xueshu jikan*, vol. 3, no.4 (1986), figure 11.

16 Zhao Zhiqian, *Yonglu xianjie*, 215.

Selected Bibliography

Ayers, John. "Chinese Glass." In *The Arts of the Ch'ing Dynasty*. Exhibition catalog. London: The Arts Council of Great Britain and the Oriental Ceramics Society, 1964.

Bushell, Stephen W. *Chinese Art*. London, 1909.

Dohrenwend, Doris. "Glass in China: A Review Based on the Collection in the Royal Ontario Museum." *Oriental Art* 26 (1980-81): 426-46.

Gabbert, Gunhild. *Chinesisches Glas*. Exhibition catalog. Frankfurt-am-Main: Museum für Kunsthandwerk, 1980.

Gan Fuxi, ed. *Zhongguo gu boli yanjiu. 1984 nian Beijing guoji boli xueshu taolunhui lunwenji* (Studies on ancient Chinese glass. Proceedings of the 1984 International Symposium, Beijing). Beijing, 1986.

Honey, William B. "Early Chinese Glass." *Burlington Magazine* 71 (1937): 211-13, 216-19 and 221-23.

———. "Chinese Glass." *Transactions of the Oriental Ceramics Society* 17 (1939-40): 35-47.

Jenyns, R. Soame. *Chinese Art III*. 2nd ed. Preface and revisions by William Watson. New York, 1981.

Mehlman, Felice. *Phaidon Guide to Glass*. Englewood Cliffs, NJ, 1983.

Needham, Joseph, et al. *Science and Civilization in China*. vol. 4, pt. 1. Cambridge, 1962.

Newman, Harold. *An Illustrated Dictionary of Glass*. London, 1977.

Plesch, Peter H. "Some Decorative Techniques Found in Later Chinese Glass." *Transactions of the Oriental Ceramics Society* 44 (1979-80): 47-66.

———. "Some Approaches to the Study of Later Chinese Glass." In *Festschrift für Peter Wilhelm Meister*. Ed. Annaliese Ohm and Horst Reber. Hamburg, 1975.

Suntory Museum of Art. *Kenryū garasu to āru nūvō* (Qianlong glass and art nouveau). Exhibition catalog. Tokyo, 1983.

Toledo Museum of Art. *Exhibition of East Asiatic Glass*. Toledo, 1948.

Warren, Phelps. "Later Chinese Glass, 1650-1900." *Journal of Glass Studies* 19 (1977): 84-126.

Yoshimizu Tsuneo and Tanahashi Junji. *Tōyō no garasu* (Far eastern glass). Tokyo, 1978.

Library of Congress Cataloging-in-Publication Data

Brown, Claudia. *The Robert H. Clague collection.* 'Exhibition sched-
ule: Phoenix Art Museum, 21 Nov - 31 Jan 1987-88; San Antonio
Museum of Art, 18 Mar - 19 Jun 1988; Suntory Museum of Art,
Tokyo, 19 Jul - 28 Aug 1988; Milwaukee Public Museum, 21 Jan -
16 Apr 1989.'

Bibliography: p.
1 Glass, Colored - China - History - Ming - Ch'ing dynasties,
1368-1912 - Exhibitions. 2 Clague, Robert - Art collections -
Exhibitions. 3 Glassware - Private collections - Arizona - Exhibitions. I Rabiner, Donald, 1949-   . II Phoenix Art Museum.
III Title.

NK5207.C6B7 1987   748.2951'074   87-42927   ISBN 0-910407-20-7